# The
# Way to Soul
# Consciousness

## A Guide to
## Personality- Soul
## Integration

David E. Hopper

Grateful acknowledgement is hereby made to the following publishers and/or copyright holders for permission to quote: Lucis Publishing Company, New York for the extracts (text and line-charts) listed in the bibliography. These extracts may not be reprinted except by permission from the Lucis Trust, which holds the copyright.

Cover designed in AI using DIY Book covers
Cover artwork by Sergio Lepore

ISBN- 9798863053806

Printed by CreateSpace in the United States of America.

# Table of Contents

# Acknowledgement

While writing this book, I realized that many of the ideas and thoughts that you are about to read are not necessarily mine. They are original in how I express them, but in truth my wisdom is a culmination of lifelong learning through many encounters with individuals and groups expressing the Ageless Wisdom. Also, and most certainly, I have to give credit to those who trod the path before me and presented their wisdom through their writings from which both you and I benefit.

As the French philosopher Bernard of Chartres wrote in the 12th century:

> "We are like dwarfs on the shoulders of giants, so that we can see more than they, and things at a greater distance, not by virtue of any sharpness of sight on our part, or any physical distinction, but because we are carried high and raised up by their giant size [and accomplishments]".

I want to acknowledge all my mentors, friends, family members, my cat, and all situations good and bad that were and are my teachers. My list also includes acknowledging Master D.K., the Alice A. Bailey and Theosophical teachings, the Arcane School and the Lucis Trust.

Special mention to my loving wife, JoAnn, who, through her patience, an as editor helped me clarify my ideas and thoughts. To Brett Mitchell for insight and philosophical support throughout the book.

# Introduction

> *"The goal of all development is integration—integration as a personality, integration with the soul, integration into the Hierarchy, integration with the Whole, until complete unity and identification has been achieved."*
>
> Alice A. Bailey, "Esoteric Healing"

This book discusses the fascinating subject of integration of the personality with the Soul. It is largely written for those people who already have or have had some sense of their spiritual identity and want to connect (or re-connect) and transform themselves on deeper levels. However, individuals with little or no former spiritual training can also benefit from this knowledge.

You may or may not be in touch directly with your Soul. Perhaps, you have a religious background and want to explore new ways of connecting with the deeper part of yourself, the Soul? Maybe you have had some experience working with your own inner self through devotion or contemplation? You can certainly benefit from this understanding. Although suggested techniques are provided, this book details various methods about how the integration process works, how you can connect with your Soul and transform your personality. Also discussed and emphasized is the idea for creating a spiritual practice. It is an ancient formula for spiritual transformation made up of meditation, spiritual study and service.

From the outset, our spiritual purpose is recognize the Soul's objective and not that of the personality. The Soul has a pure nature made up of Divine love and intelligence. When you are able to connect with it and allow its higher vibrations to transform your personality, you then can make spiritual progress. Over numerous lifetimes the Soul seeks to infuse its higher will via impression. An impression is composed of light and love projected from the Soul into the mental, emotional and physical bodies of your personality.

We will explore how the personality develops through these aspects and how it learns to work in the world with intelligent loving or "love-wisdom".

As a personality, you express the "light" through intelligence, wisdom, purpose, and love. Light also describes your true nature as a luminous being. Working with the Soul in this way, the personality must learn to cooperate by controlling how thought and feeling are expressed in your daily life. Over time, you will build and achieve a balance between the mental, emotional, and physical bodies and with the Soul. Successful integration of the personality will shed light through all your activities, problems and life's encounters, thus rendering greater Soulful service. This ultimately creates a coordinated instrument to become sensitive to energies emanating from the Soul and other higher spiritual sources. This work becomes the "Lighted Way".

By definition the integration of the personality with the Soul is a "mental" process. In this book you are encouraged to work as an esotericist, i.e. who "knows" about energy (thoughts and emotion) and forces (the will). This is not to say that the emotions are not involved. Indeed, the emotional body is a major topic of concern as it must become a reflector of the love and intelligence of the Soul. This and many ideas are presented in showing you that the process of integration requires constant effort to train your mind and emotions to become this mirror of higher thought and expression.

An integration in consciousness will manifest as a "blending" of energies of the Soul with those of the personality. You will come to understand why you will want to "eliminate" or let go of that which is not of a higher vibration and allow you to dwell in the natural state of consciousness and awareness. Overcoming hinderances and blocks allows you to achieve clear seeing of the Self in its natural state. By building in the higher values and qualities, e.g. goodwill and harmlessness your personality will transform.

As an esotericist, you will learn to train yourself to be consciously sensitive to impression and allow the higher vibrations to become part of your everyday life.

The Ageless Wisdom Teachings tells us that the highest form of love manifests in two forms, through the energies of wisdom and compassion. When Love is expressed through wisdom we have understanding in the mind. With compassion we have the feeling of love or empathy through the heart.

Consciously implementing the energies of "love-wisdom" will help you to become an esotericist, working consciously with matter and energy. Additionally, as much as you evolve yourself with the Soul, then you will sense change within. You will have a "new" perspective for communicating and sharing with others..

Your journey is learning about *who and what you are* as a spiritual being. Its also a story of evolution and how you can become aware of your greater spiritual essence, the Soul. Using the metaphor of unpeeling an onion, you must remove all mental or emotional obstacles in consciousness to discover your true nature at the core of your being.

In this work, you will learn to turn desire into aspiration and to contact the world of Soul through meditation. In the early stages of Soul integration, you may have emotional or devotional aspiration, but not know how to go deeper. The teaching presented here is to learn and trust opening your heart and mind, and not be limited. This provides glimpses of the light of the Soul where you obtain knowledge and meaning. As your mind learns to become "steady" in that light, you learn to identify and become that "light". You will discover during the process of purification as you clear away the blockages, you can work consciously and cooperatively with your Soul in your service work.

In short, this book is written *not as the only means towards enlightenment.* Yes it is set up to "streamline the process of integration" but it should be said, there are no shortcuts on the spiritual path. You must do the work by clearing away anything that keeps you from fully realizing your true spiritual Self – the Soul. I will say that what I describe is a tried and true efficient process which will enable a considerable amount of Soul integration. I describe many ideas and understandings for training your mind to become awake. This is about becoming an esotericist who is aware of the energies an forces in his nature and learns to weld them.

If you apply the suggestions, processes and techniques, you will expand your consciousness and move towards integrating your personality with the Soul. It is up to you as to how deep you want to go and achieve.

**A Personal and Planetary Awakening**

In the Ageless Wisdom teachings, the Macrocosm, manifesting as the Solar Logos, is from the point of view of all living things, it is God to everything within the solar system. From this great Being love and intelligence conditions humanity by Its manifested will, love and intelligence or the Trinity: Christianity as Father, Son, Holy Ghost. In Hinduism as Shiva, Vishnu Brahma. The primary purpose of the Logos is to evolve by ensconcing cosmic love and intelligence into the minds or consciousness of all human beings.

We as Humanity are in the process of becoming the first generation to awaken to be "conscious of its own consciousness". This means people are waking up and realizing they can shape their own destiny for the better instead of by manipulation. We are awakening to an awareness that we are "One" with all that breathes. If that is so, then we must protect the physical environment for future generations and cultivate a mindset that generates cooperation, and a loving attitude towards people and the environment. First, we must transform ourselves individually and extend that higher wisdom to the greater collective Humanity.

For the individual and group, awakening refers to a stimulation on the inner "subjective" world where we have our feelings, thoughts, ideas, motivations and dreams. There are people across the world, whether they are conscious of it or not, who are stimulated by ideas and impressions. These emanate from spiritual Teachers, Guides, inspired thinkers and information that causes them to be influenced on the mental and emotional levels.

Awakening is a time for those who are sensitive to these impulses to become aware of the interconnectedness and interdependence we have with each other, our community and with all the kingdoms of Nature.

With this awakening awareness, we see how politicians can work with economists with scientists, with educators, people of faith, the healing profession, the Arts and those who are presenting "ideas and information" to the public.

This awakening is causing an increasing number of individuals and groups to simultaneously awaken and become aware and make sense of the happenings in the World. We must ask:

- *Why go this path? What can you achieve?*
- *Why is this path the most efficient?*
- *How long will it take to achieve Illumination?*

This book attempts to directly answer these questions by discussing the process you are undertaking and using mental techniques.

# How to Use this Book

The Way to Soul Consciousness details processes of how you can initiate personal transformation within your own consciousness and become a "Soul Integrated Personality". It is designed to be practical at the most basic level. (See the Glossary for a definition of the Soul).

I am inviting you to become mindful, consciously aware of yourself in every possible way.

On the face of it, I describe many aspects of the heart, the mind, and the personality and how to transform your consciousness. I strive to make the teachings in the various sections come alive, but It is up to you to apply the information, set your own pace and implement that activity in your life.

The first part of the book describes the energy of love and its various manifestations. Love is truly at the core of our being. Because of love (whether you are conscious of it or not) much of our actions, be it physical, verbal and emotional are motivated from this core energy. Connecting with the Soul's nature will show who you are and who you are not and certainly what you may be.

The chapter "Approach to Spirituality" describes how you can put yourself in a space for listening  and observing within. For this work, it is necessary that you begin learning to consciously know what you are doing at any moment as your are expanding your awareness.

By becoming observant and mindful you prepare yourself for "consciously" moving into a conscious and spiritual space. An overview of the Integration process is described.

The "Hierarchy and the Masters" chapter talks about the Spiritual Hierarchy as Guides for Humanity. As Custodians of the Plan, their intent to transform Humanity in practicing right human relations in both the inner and outer planes. Through Their great sacrifice, love and wisdom Humanity is guided in evolving ourselves individually and civilization as a whole. The planetary Hierarchy, also called the Masters of the Wisdom collectively manifest love through all its activities. The Hierarchy identifies with unity and oneness of all creation. Its purpose, as it descends into the world of individual and group souls, is to facilitate the evolution all Souls.

The highest expression of love is "love-wisdom" or love expressed and radiated through full consciousness awareness in life's activities.

When expressed in this way, wisdom conditions the individual to become the "knower" at the deepest levels of the mind.

The chapter "Human Constitution" describes your basic physical-etheric, emotional and mental nature. This will provide an important foundation of knowledge prior to integration about the whole self, including what the Soul is wanting to transform and become. Details about the lower 3-Fold nature are described.

The main chapter for this book is "Building Towards Integration". Just as the title chapter suggests, it is about the integration process and how to implement change within. Also outlined are the various stages of transformation around the purification process. This revolves around refining the mental and emotional bodies, learning the importance of becoming the Observer in consciousness, and transcending the influence of glamour, illusion and maya. It is for you as the "conscious" individual, i.e. the "esotericist" to learn to employ numerous methods and use techniques to become serious and knowledgeable about transforming your inner planes reality. This will allow you to make the best and most efficient progress.

Note, when using the term "esotericist", it denotes the individual who is relatively awake and conscious of his thoughts and activities.

Reference materials in the back of the book:

- Appendices:
    - A - Techniques for Working in Consciousness;
    - B - Stages of Discipleship;
    - C - Attributes, Virtues and Glamours of the 7 Rays
- Glossary of Terms - definitions used in the book.
- Bibliography

David E. Hopper, February, 2024

# Approach to Spirituality

An "Awakening" Within

There comes a lifetime when you may sense something within your consciousness that is greater than your self. Perhaps, you are sensing the Soul, a higher Being or even Divinity Itself? When this happens, you awaken to something greater than your life of trouble and difficulties that many in the human family share. It is a time for discovering how the Greater Self, (which we are calling the Soul) expresses and influences you in so many ways, while acting as a background of consciousness. *Why does the Soul need to do this?* It is your personality that is incarnated by the Soul with one primary purpose, to expand your consciousness and eventually evolve into a sense of oneness or unity with the Divine. To get to this point in awareness you must clear away anything that blocks you from a direct connection with the Divine.

Although the teaching described here is based on a Theosophical perspective and other Ageless Wisdom sources, it invites people from all beliefs and backgrounds to learn about the spiritual Self. If you happen to have previous religious training, maybe a mystical or a religious experience and you want to "know" what it means, or even want to deepen the experience, this teachings can work for you.

While these experiences may stimulate your interest it is recommended for you not to let attachments, such as to religious dogma, or the limitation of a particular teaching keep you from learning a new way to connect with your authentic Divine Self. By embracing a "spiritual attitude" and desire to want to connect deeper with your Greater Self, this approach will take you further on the path of discovery and eventual liberation.

You may ask:

*Why go this path? What can I spiritually achieve?*

*How long will it take to achieve Illumination or a connection with God or the Divine?*

For lifetimes the incarnating personality treads the path of acquiring experience and understanding. Through all sorts of interactions, encounters, and situations on the physical plane, the separated personality immerses itself in experience. After lifetimes of acquired experience, the Soul desires to learn and evolve through its lower correspondence, the personality. From the experiences of the personality, it is ultimately the Soul that gains understanding, and eventually wisdom.

As much as you grow and expand your awareness, you deepen your connection with the Soul and will be able to answer the questions of *"Who am I?"* and *"What is my Purpose?"* In time, you will come to understand on a deeper level that you are on a spiritual path that reveals life's meaning and purpose.

One of the early injunctions is for the aspirant (one who aspires) to understand the concept of *"know thyself"*. This concept is important as he needs to know who he is at the personality level and how he expresses Soul qualities in the world. If he does not know himself, he will potentially wander around blindly and recklessly, and expend energy without thought or lack of direction.

Another reason why the personality incarnates is to obtain the Soul's vantage point and offset lifetimes of negative experiences or karma. When connected with the Soul, your personality can express the good, loving service, cooperation and goodwill through your many human activities and situations with other people. Through positive encounters with people and groups, the Soul acquires wisdom from each life.

The Objective vs. Subjective Realities

For the vast majority of people in our materialistic-focused civilization, life revolves around the 5 senses and the rational-concrete thinking states. The individual acts as a "separated personality" and sees the overt or exoteric world of objectivity as "the truth" and the only reality. His connection with the Soul is weak or not part of his awareness.

In the objective reality, he interacts with the world via his personality and physical body-form nature through the expression of his own ideas, perspectives, biases, interpretations, opinions, and feelings.

For the spiritual seeker, the subjective or "inner world" is seen as the source where thought and impressions emanate from the Soul. These act as a force that influences the individual's mind. Know that the lower mind is made up of the concrete and rational thinking mind, whereas the Soul is the highest part of the mind. It consists of the abstract mind and has a direct connection with manas and the Spiritual Triad. (See Chapter: "Human Constitution" for definition).

Initially, when contact with the Soul begins, the individual is inspired with a sense of duty and responsibility. For the spiritual seeker, the connection with the Soul helps him develop a fine sense of discrimination and he learns to distinguish between energy (thoughts and feelings) and force (the will) as the subjective energies of the Soul impinge on his consciousness.

Over time, the individual's awareness becomes fine tuned. He comes to know the difference between how he uses his mind, his thoughts and freewill as a force. Its also knowing the difference of the energies coming from the Soul as an influence.

**The Divine Plan for Humanity**

The Ageless Wisdom Teachings present an understanding that Divine inspiration comes from solar and cosmic sources.

This 'inspiration' is a type of knowledge and energy that is stepped down into what is called the 'Plan'.

The Plan is a blueprint or energy formula expressing light, love and the will-to-good for humanity and all kingdoms. In its most basic form it is a thought expressing the 3 major Divine aspects working out in Humanity - Namely: Will, Love and Active Intelligence.

The *Plan for Humanity* is guided by group of advanced Souls or ascended Masters who just like us have suffered, and incarnated on Earth. However, they eventually achieved liberation from the physical plane and the cycle of rebirth. They are called the Hierarchy and act as custodians of God's Plan for working out on Earth. The Christ and Buddha are part of the Hierarchy including numerous other members, e.g. Masters, Sages, Mystics and Saints from all cultures, religions and beliefs over the Ages.

The Hierarchy, as custodians of the Plan provide a blueprint for personal and planetary evolution by conveying it to spiritual seekers, via impressions. An impression is registered the same way you *"get an impression"* of something or somebody. It is often associated with inspiration, guidance, impulse, incentive, influence, and aspiration. It acts as an idea, stimulation, energy or force communicated to the individual's consciousness.

In all cultures and nations around the world, individuals are interpreting the Plan through their activities by practicing higher values, e.g. goodwill, cooperation, and harmlessness through thought and action. Although impressions are never imposed, individuals and humanity as a whole must learn to become "conscious agents" in human evolution while enabling God's Plan.

Eventually, the energies of cooperation and goodwill will be a primary expression in all human affairs. This will ensure a world and civilization maintained through mutual benefit, not by an imposed authority, or a utopian dream. In short, by combining the Heart and mind in this way, this is a major expression of the Plan for our stage of evolution.

**Journey of the Soul**

The Ageless Wisdom Teachings describe the journey of the Soul beginning through a process called *individualization*. This involved "imparting the spark of mind" or thinking capacity into man. In the beginning, this spark gave man the first sense of the separate "I". He existed for untold lifetimes with no particular purpose except to acquire experience and a measure of understanding about who and what he is. The spark of mind initially drove man's instinct to work with the material form of the physical plane.

Until that point the mind of man was spiritually undeveloped and only had physical appetites. He was animal-man.

Over the eons humans evolved from the strictly physical and emotional existence to where we are today. Man is still emotional, but his mind has evolved to be capable of integrating the highest aspects of his nature with the Soul, ultimately with the pure Spirit known in Eastern teachings as the Monad. The Soul as neither spirit nor matter relates spirit and matter together and acts a vehicle or 'agent' of the pure Spirit. This journey, covering hundreds of lifetimes is about establishing consciousness awareness with that pure Spirit throughout all planes on the Cosmic Physical Plane.

The Soul is made up of the mind, the vital-etheric body, and the emotional nature. The physical body is an automaton in which the personality lives and interacts with the physical plane.

At the Soul level, it can simultaneously manifest as individualistic and universal. It transfers the principles of sentiency and intelligence to its lesser reflection of the incarnating man, the personality. This is demonstrated through his mind and mental awareness, which gives man the power to discriminate and analyze activities on the physical plane. From this, his personality gains experience and progresses on the path of development through impulses by the Soul.

When the mind of man is sufficiently developed, the mind has two expressions - the lower concrete mind and the higher spiritual or abstract mind. The concrete mind allows the personality to analyze and discriminate and connect with all expressions and kingdoms of the physical plane. The abstract mind, as a part of man's higher mental nature and a connection with the Soul permits him to comprehend the principles of universal brotherhood, synthesis, and absolute unity.

When enough of the higher energy of mind, awareness and sentiency permeates the lower personality, it produces a vibration so potent that there is a fusion of the higher spirit and matter. The result is the blending of life, body, quality and appearance through the tangible human form.

Man's spiritual development and expanded consciousness is facilitated through life experiences. The Soul provides man with a sense of continuity between successive incarnations. From each life, the personality gains experience and it learns how to love like the Soul. For the conscious spiritual seeker, he practices what is called in esotericism "love-wisdom". Eventually, he consciously evolves to a place where he is living a divinely embodied life, and in so doing helps others do the same. Thus, he is intentionally participating in his own evolution.

Nearing the end of the Soul's journey, it in combination with the personality will embark on what is called the Path of Liberation. Here the term "Liberation" has a two-fold meaning.

It refers to liberation from the influence of physical substance or matter. In other words, it is liberation from the desire nature of the personality that seeks to only stay focused on objects, the desire for them, and phenomena of the physical plane. Liberation also has to do with fully recognizing our true spiritual nature which is that of pure Spirit, i.e. the Monad.

For you the spiritual seeker, the path of liberation is a path where you eventually choose to wake up and become conscious of your thoughts, your feelings and actions. In this process you learn to let go of the pulls and influences of the lower planes and learn to create an "at-onement" with the Soul.

A major objective of the Soul is to replace the lower energies of the 3-Fold personality, i.e. the physical, emotional-astral, and mental planes with is corresponding energies of the Spiritual Triad, i.e. Atma, Buddhi, and Manas. This enables the consciousness of the personality to expand and evolve. It is an evolutionary process for change that you are learning to be "consciously" part of. Once connected with the Soul, performing service is a natural expression towards fulfilling the Soul's purpose.

It should be noted that religious and spiritual traditions have a very different view on the existence of a Soul. Buddhism sees the Soul as a creation of the mind. Although Christianity or Judaism acknowledges the Soul, they do not recognize the concept of our innate Divinity.

In this philosophy and understanding, man is and always has had a divine nature. It's the long journey of awakening to this fact and discovering what the process of awakening is about.

## Stages of Integration (Overview)

Think of two circles. One is the personality, the other the Soul. Throughout out numerous incarnations, the personality circle stays separate and largely unconscious of the Soul.

Then comes a lifetime where the Soul wishes to bring the personality into an at-onement, hence a merging process ensues. At this time, the two circles begin to overlap and blend, especially during the probationary and discipleship phases. A final integration culminates during initiation where the two circles become one.

A high level understanding of the integration process can be described in the following stages.

Alignment: the spiritual seeker will follow a prescribed idea of connecting with the Soul through meditation. The Soul responds via impression and the individual begins the alignment of the lower three bodies, i.e. the mental, emotional-astral and the physical-etheric. Alignment is bringing all three bodies into a realized oneness. The individual then seeks a greater alignment of the 3-fold personality and creates an at-onement with the Soul.

Light: The individual enters into a phase of light and awareness where he sees clearly the next steps for him to take. He is passing through a process of reorientation.

Crisis: During the alignment process the subtle energies of the Soul will create a crisis in the personality. The crisis is in the form of purification where anything that is not of the Soul, e.g. anger, hate, over-reaching desire, etc. must be brought under control. For the spiritually conscious individual crisis is not a disaster but an opportunity for removing all hinderances or obstacles that block Soul contact.

Revelation: With an established alignment with the Soul and a purging of obstacles the individual is open to a sense of revelation of the Plan and his potential connection with it from the Soul.

Integration: This is the process of fully integrating all three bodies into a relational whole with the Soul. It marks a time of fusion whereby the conscious thinker comes to awareness that integration is both desirable and can be achieved. He wants to contribute and not acquire. Deeper levels of integration progressively occur into the family unit, the nation and the social order of humanity. He can function as a World Server.

From this, the integration process is both sensed in his physical nature, but also becomes an attitude of mind. Spiritual man realizes his relational part with the Whole but also his inter-relation with all parts of the Whole. For an individual who has awakened in this manner, he has taken a major step on the Path of Return.

➤ Note, the Stages of Integration will be discussed in greater detail in chapter "Building Towards Integration".

## Light and Illumination

When speaking of light, we understand that Light is indicative of how much Soul dominance exists in the personality. In his early stages, man's sense of the Soul's light was dim. Initially, he was aware of the physical light of the sun for seeing and for warmth. He learned to use artificial light to illuminate areas where there was darkness, and thereby allowing for the light of knowledge to work out.

Later, man became unconsciously attracted to other subtle forms of light. As he expanded his awareness, he became aware of the light in his mind. His recognitions have evolved through four main sources of light:

1. Light of Instinct. Instinct is associated with the animal stage prior to reasoning or thinking.

2. Light of Knowledge. This relates to educating the everyday man to allow him to become "consciously aware". Knowledge is a product of the concrete mind and is an

impulse that brings light or understanding to areas of consciousness that are in darkness. This type of light has dispelled glamours through the light of mind.

3. Light of Wisdom. This is the light of the Soul. It is the sum of learned experiences combined with knowledge. This light involves illumination of subjective realms of meaning or reality to propel the spiritual seeker on the Path of Light and expanded awareness.

   The Light of the Soul reveals a relationship existing between the real and the unreal, and the nature of the formless life to the phenomenal.

   From this level of consciousness, light of the Soul brings awareness towards synthesis and group expression.

4. Light of Intuition. When the spiritual worker begins building the Antakarana (a bridge between the personality and Soul) using the abstract mind, a pathway to the Buddhic Plane opens up. From it flows the intuition and pure reason.

   This indicates a blending of the Soul light with that of the Monad and reveals to him the life of Divinity.

   ➤ Note, a detailed description and purpose of the the Antakarana is described in chapter "Building Towards Integration", "Antakarana – Building the Bridge of Light".

Light in the Head

The light in the head or illumination refers to an interplay between the Soul, the spiritual man, and his lesser 3-Fold nature. When this occurs, the light of the Soul force allows the individual to combine instinct, intellect and intuition through the will in facilitating his own spiritual evolution.

The light in the head is indicative of several factors:

- Upon first Soul contact, the pineal gland in the head is stimulated into activity. Establishing contact can be through meditation, mental control of thoughts and feelings, and allowing an inflow of spiritual force from the Soul to condition the 3-Fold nature of the personality.

- Alignment of man's lesser mind, feelings and desires on the physical plane. This eventually allows the physical plane life to be brought under the control of the Soul.

- Downflow of spiritual force via sutratma (i.e. life force) from the Soul to the mind.

  This enables spiritual vision, correct perception and right contact. This downflow is indicative of the stream of illumination into the brain.

- The light in the head will bring to the foreground of consciousness any thoughts or energies that depict the lower life or darkness in his being.

- Finding the Path. The spiritual seeker should study and acquire an understanding of how the light is centralized, intensified, and entered.
  It is recommended the light should *"be followed back until the source of the lower manifestation is reached and the Soul consciousness is entered"*.

# Methods of Transformation

In the following sections of this chapter are descriptions of some of the most important elements that make up the integration process. Its not enough to just meditate or devote your life to a spiritual practice, or even seek at-onement with your greater Self. While you are in the process of integrating the lesser self with the Soul, you will come to see yourself differently and your capacity for understanding and going within will deepen. Having knowledge about the dynamics of the self (personality) and integrating with the Higher Self (Soul) can be very valuable for progressing in your spiritual work.

**Principles and Laws Govern Man**

A principle represents a fundamental truth acting as the foundation for a system of belief or behavior or for a line of thinking. The key word here is "foundation" as it provides a way for esoteric understanding of a higher truth that ultimately invokes the quality of love and unity in your consciousness.

It also describes the basic qualities or types of energy which embodies some aspect of the divine unfolding consciousness being developed upon each of the seven planes and subplanes on the cosmic physical plane. From this understanding, a principle holds a kernel of awareness and allows for sensitivity and divine understanding and makes possible knowledge and conscious response to an environment.

For man, there are principles that evoke a response related to the human form as it evolves. For example, from each plane of the Cosmic Physical Plane, principles are developing and working out in man.

- Physical plane: Prana: vital energy and etheric body
- Emotional-Astral plane: desire, feeling, love, astral body
- Mental plane:
  - o Lower manas: Concrete mind
  - o Higher manas: abstract mind, Soul / Causal body
- Intuitional / Buddhic Plane: Buddhi: intuition, pure reason, pure love, wisdom
- Monadic: 3 Aspects of Divinity, i.e. Will, Love-Wisdom, Intelligence

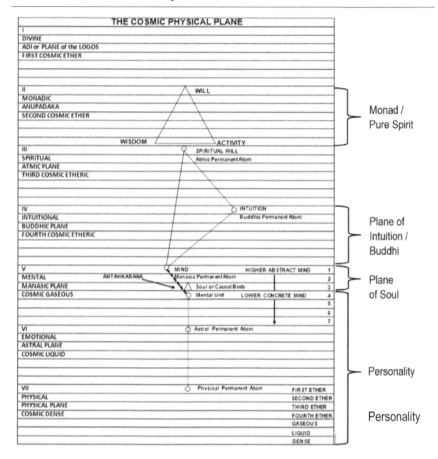

Note, the human body is not a principle but an instrument of the Soul which "responds" to the energies of prana, kama, manas, and buddhi.

Within society, there are two basic kinds of principles acting out, governing man's behavior.

1 – Principles governing man's lower personal self in dealing with actions in his worldly life. These are enacted within society through laws and commandments, e.g. Thou shalt not kill, steal, etc.

- Here man learns that to steal, he suffers pain and learns to steal no more.

- From this first postulate, the general public must be educated towards the recognition of awakening deep-seated qualities of the Soul and higher. The lower principles deal with the good of the individual.

Principles governing the lower personal self deal with personal actions in everyday life. They control the individuals life during times of rash and inconsiderate behavior and provide rules for living with concern for others. These principles provide the basis for the 10 Commandments, and the equivalent existing in all religions and cultures. "Thou shall not kill, steal, or covet", etc. are principles that exist on the physical, emotional-astral and lower mental planes.

> *"The lower activity of the separate individual, regardless of how good or worthy, must eventually be transcended by the higher love life that seeks the good of the group and not the unit".*
>
> Alice A. Bailey, "A Treatise on White Magic"

From these laws and commandments, man learns through pain after having created disaster in his life and others. Humanity is learning these hard lessons at both the individual and group level.

2 – Principles governing the higher Self or Soul that deal with the love-wisdom aspect and truths effecting the good of the group in all human affairs.

It is inferred that the individual takes to heart the "commandments" for the lower self that society mandates. It is the higher principles that the everyday person is now beginning to apprehend. At the level of ethics, the individual applying a higher wisdom in consciousness and life's activities would be accountable, transparent, and beyond corruption. Examples of these are respect for all cultures, minorities, genders, sexual orientation and living a life of ethics. Thus "he is transparent and accountable in his rhetoric and activities."

When man's emotional plane is controlled via the intuitional plane, then this principle will be fulfilled.

Other examples of the "lower and higher" principle working out, an individual should love his family is a statement of principle governing the individual personality. Later, he will become aware and transmute this more "limited from of love" into a greater principle of love for his fellow man at the group level, such as love for the greater community, nation and humanity. When the emotional-astral plane representing desire and separatism is dominated by the energy of buddhi coming from the Intuitional Plane, a major step forward will be accomplished.

Those who have a sense of bringing forth a vision of synthesis and unity, provide the basis of bringing forth the higher principles of love and wisdom. Examples can be individuals within an organization who sacrifice themselves "on a principle" that in reality is a principle that governs the personality life. Another example of this might be a company's Vision Statement that sells products derived from "certified organic sources". In order to fulfill the vision statement, the CEO down to the lowest employee must all adhere to their basic fundamental principle.

# The Hierarchy and the Masters

The Hierarchy is that group of advanced Souls that make up the Kingdom of Souls. They have no individual or separated awareness. While they posses sight, hearing, thought, and experience, there is no separate "I" or egoic consciousness creating that awareness. Through their efforts, they eventually became liberated Masters of the Wisdom and of the 49 planes of the Cosmic Physical Plane.

This group consists of Masters, Adepts, and Initiates working through their disciples. The Christ and Buddha are members of the Hierarchy and it includes thousands of other members, including saints and sages who were part of all cultures, religions and beliefs over the Ages.

These elder beings are characterized by love, compassion and wisdom, acquired over millennia and lifetimes. They have awakened to their own true nature and seek to help mankind also achieve that goal. At one time, they too had bodies and lives that wrestled with the dangers, sorrows, and pains of everyday living. As they struggled to master the physical, emotional-astral and mental planes, they triumphed over the influence of matter, its addictions, and the cycle of rebirth.

A major purpose of the Hierarchy is to act as "way-showers" who present knowledge and wisdom by demonstrating a new understanding of the Soul and Spirit.

The Hierarchy of Masters act as custodians of the Plan. They are only concerned with unfolding the Plan as it deals with the overall picture in how it is affecting nations, political structures, world religions, and the progressive evolution of world affairs. The Plan is framed around the free-will of Humanity. Spiritually sensitive individuals are expressing loving understanding, and goodwill in service-related activities continue their efforts towards implementing "right human relations" in all fields of human endeavor.

Hierarchical objectives for Humanity are:

1. Raise the level of human consciousness so intelligent thinking people will be consciously in touch with the world of ideas and the realm of intuitive perception.
2. Clarification of international situations. This refers to a nation's importance attending to their own business and promoting order, peace, economic stabilization and beautification of the national life in their own country.
3. Growth of a group idea with an emphasis on group good, group understanding, group interrelation, and group goodwill.

Djwhal Kuhl ('Master D.K., i.e. The Tibetan') is a Master of the Wisdom. He is said to be the source of teachings known as the Ageless Wisdom representing the 2$^{nd}$ dispensation of spiritual wisdom characterized by "love-wisdom". From 1919-1949, He worked with Alice A. Bailey as his amanuensis in a 30-year collaboration from his telepathic dictation.

Bailey's work was considered to be the second of three dispensations of the spiritual wisdom laying a foundation for the New Age or Age of Aquarius. D.K. was the Master who also inspired and guided Helena P. Blavatsky while writing the "Secret Doctrine" as the 1$^{st}$ dispensation of spiritual wisdom. This book and teaching formed the basis of the Theosophical Movement.

Although man plays a major part in the evolution of the Divine Plan, he is guided by his Soul, whether consciously, or unconsciously. When humanity begins to transmit the light and spiritual potency to the lower mineral, plant and animal kingdoms, this will create a communication between the Hierarchy, and the Plan.

It is only at the 3rd Initiation that the disciple-initiate has his first clear glimpse of the Plan as he is directly infused by the Monad. When that happens, he will have direct knowledge of the Plan with his thoughts and ideas directly impressed by the Monad.

As custodians of the Plan, the Hierarchy's chief responsibilities are:

- Work constantly at the task of awakening the consciousness aspect in all forms, in all kingdoms.

- The Hierarchy only works through individuals and groups whose ideas and attitudes are inclusive, non-critical and non-separative. These people will typically be disciples, men and women of goodwill.

# The Human Constitution

In this brief overview of your human constitution, each aspect of the 3-Fold personality and its importance will be examined in detail as it transforms through the integration process.

The Human Constitution is a living energy system bridging 7 planes and 7 subplanes of the Cosmic Physical Plane. In all, it comprises the physical form, the etheric vehicle, the astral vehicle, the lesser mental, the permanent atoms, the abstract mind, the Causal Body (Soul), the Spiritual Triad (atma, buddhic, manas), and the Monad. A discussion of the human constitution is about the evolution of consciousness through the personality and its 3 personality bodies, taking place over multiple lifetimes.

**Evolution through the Personality Bodies**

In Theosophical and Eastern spiritual teachings, human evolution is understood as bringing the 3-fold personality, i.e. physical, emotional and mental into an alignment and integration with its higher correspondence the atma-buddhi-manas of the Spiritual Triad.

For the spiritual seeker, the 3 bodies provide a means for directly developing awareness of the Soul. As much as the mental, emotional and physical bodies are purified, then the Soul is provided with better bodies for its light to be registered and perform service.

Under the guidance of the Soul, spiritual man has undergone numerous experiences and life situations, and eventually learns, acquires wisdom, and evolves using his three bodies of expression. In this process, he becomes a "Soul Integrated Personality". Finally, passing through numerous transforms he merges with the Monad to have full conscious awareness at the lowest expression of matter of the Cosmic physical plane.

The 3-Fold personality is expressed through the 3 Bodies of Expression:

- Physical-etheric
- Emotional – Astral Body
- Mind

**Physical-Etheric body**

The Physical-Etheric body is composed of a dense, physical substance, a nervous system, the glands, a brain, and a vitality / energy system from the Soul. The dense physical body is formed by the matter of the lowest three subplanes of the physical plane. The etheric body is formed of the four highest or etheric subplanes of the physical plane.

- The physical form is a vehicle for the personality to have experience on the physical plane. Its health and vitality are maintained through right hygiene, regular diet, and exercise.

- The man in incarnation is a Soul, who posses a body through which he has experience on the physical plane.

- The Etheric Body is the energy or 'vital' vehicle, which interpenetrates and corresponds to the dense physical body. It is a finer level of matter than the dense physical form and has 7 major energy centers or chakras.

The etheric body is made up of chakras or energy centers. During an incarnation, the personality is given life in the dense physical world via the "sutratma" or life thread. Originating from the Monad, the Soul acts as a conduit for this life energy as it provides the physical form with the will to live.

These energy centers interpenetrate and occupy the entire physical organism. It receives and distributes force from many different directions, e.g. from prana, impressions from the abstract mind or Soul, psychic impressions or thoughts, and from others through telepathy. The centers are focal points of energy located in the etheric body.

They act as transmitters of certain forms of energy consciously directed by the Soul with the intent of driving the physical body to fulfilling the Soul's purpose. The everyday man is largely functioning through the solar plexus center. This is a process that transfers energy and force from the centers below the diaphragm to the centers above the solar plexus. The whole process is one of development, use and transference.

The etheric body is a reflection of the Soul of man. It links the physical form with the higher Atma, the astral - emotional body with buddhi of the Intuitional Plane, and the mental to manas of the spiritual triad. When the individual becomes completely Soul-infused, connections can become possible to the higher planes in the solar system.

It is instructive for the aspirant to study the forces and energies which interact through the etheric field and cause the physical form, the brain and consciousness to be energized into action. The Spiritual worker should learn to subjugate the emotional body, develop his mental powers, and cultivate the faculty of abstract thinking. These actions will over time achieve positive results upon the etheric body, and thus eliminate any premature awakening of the centers and contribute to increased health of the whole 3-Fold nature..

When the disciple achieves a measure of Soul-integration, man will be governed from the head center.

Chakras - Centers of Energy

"Chakra" is Sanskrit term for energy vortice or wheel.

The etheric body has 7 major chakras or energy centers and nadis, each of which gives man vitality, energy and life and effects the physiology of the physical body.

The centers correspond approximately to the nervous system, and have an effect on the glands of the endocrine system. They control the physical organs, all of which maintain life processes.

The major Centers or Chakras are:

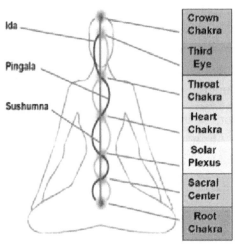

- Crown: Brain; Connection with Divine;

- Third Eye: Pineal gland, or Ajna;

- Throat: Thyroid gland, Bronchial tubes, Lungs, and Vocal cords;

- Heart: Thymus gland for the immune system;

- Solar Plexus: Pancreas, Liver, Stomach;

- Sacral: Gonads, Reproductive system;

- Root: Adrenal glands.

The energy centers are overlaid and connected to the physical body through the 'sutratma' or life thread in the Heart. They are all stimulated by the Soul at periodic intervals in the aspirant's life. This facilitates an alignment in the lower mental, emotional, and physical nature in order to bring personality into a coherent and functioning unit.

The seven centers are not within the dense physical body but exist only in etheric matter, overlaying the physical form.

## Nadis – Carriers of Energy

Within the etheric body, an extensive network of tiny lines of force called *nadis* exist. Nadis is a Sanskrit term describing a network of channels of subtle and cosmic, vital, and mental energies, or *prana* that flow between the centers. Subtle stimulation can also emanate from the Soul.

The nadis are important for the function of consciousness, sensations and the human aura. In the etheric body they are the etheric correspondence to the human nervous system, such as cerebro-spinal, sympathetic and peripheral.

Through these lines of force or vital energies, the quality of the system is nourished and controlled. Additionally, they are related to the seven major chakras and the spinal column with the head.

Although the nadis are of a physical substance, they are of a finer and subtler matter than the nervous system. If one has clairvoyant vision and could see the entire etheric body, it would appear as a human Christmas tree with all the force centers and nadis radiating various colors.

When the aspirant's consciousness begins to expand, three main channels in the etheric body come into play:

- Ida

- Pingala

- Sushumna

The Ida and Pingala are found up the spine on each side of the central channel, the Sushumna. The consciously aware disciple using the intuition and under the direction of the Soul can willfully move energies up and down these etheric channels. See chakra diagram.

Their purpose is to allow Soul force to hasten the burning away of any remaining etheric webs or blockages surrounding any center. This usually happens nearing the final stages of the aspirant's evolution.

The nadis originate from the heart center and the pelvic area, just below the navel. The Ida and Pingala nadis are sometimes in modern readings interpreted as the two hemispheres of the brain.

- Ida is the introverted nadi and corresponds to the left hand side of the body and the right side of the brain.

- Pingala is the nadi corresponding to the right-hand side of the body and the left side of the brain.

Certain pranayama breathing techniques are practiced to direct the flow of prana within these nadis causing extrasensory function, e.g. empathic and instinctive. This would involve breathing through either the left and right nostrils, which would possibly stimulate either the left and right sides of the brain. Accordingly, these techniques can purify and develop these two energetic currents and may lead to the awakening of kundalini.

Kundalini

Kundalini, also called the 'Serpent of Power' is an evolutionary force within each individual. It can be described as a "fiery power" that lies coiled in etheric matter at the base of the human spine. When drawn up through the centers, such as through breathing exercises, it will activate the chakras, and stimulate them into activity.

Note: Working directly with the kundalini energy can have a direct effect on the vital body and etheric centers. If the individual tries to deliberately awaken internal forces within himself without the aid of a trusted teacher, this can cause harm to the unsuspecting person in the mental and emotional nature.

If the evolutionary fires are prematurely awakened anywhere in the etheric body without proper training, such as through certain breathing techniques, or by raising the kundalini, then the person could possibly suffer dangerous consequences on the mental, emotional, or physical-etheric levels. For example, if there is a focus below the diaphragm then the sex life and astral plane can be over stimulated. If the focus is above the diaphragm then egotism, heart disease, emotionalism, and problems with the brain, pituitary, and thyroid glands can ensue.

Most teachings, regardless of culture, wisely encourage the student to *make haste slowly,* or to practice moderation in the spiritual practice. The science of esotericism is *not* concerned with awakening the centers, or using certain breathing exercises to awaken or move the kundalini.

Premature Awakening of the Centers

When impurities exist in the life of the aspirant, the premature awakening of the centers can result in unstable mental, emotional and physical health. Instead, it is recommended to allow the centers to develop and unfold slowly as the aspirant disciplines himself and allows the Soul to guide the personality life.

The exception to this rule might be to allow the heart center to become energized in the early stages of spiritual development. Its important to express intelligent loving activity in life's activities and interactions. In esotericism, this is called "love-wisdom". At this time, the aspirant learns to become group conscious, sensitive to group ideals and not be driven by personality attraction, ambition, motive or reward. Under the Soul's guidance, he can wield the creative powers of the throat center for higher purposes.

**Endocrine Glands: Physical Body and Human Behavior**

In every human being there are seven major centers or chakras making up the etheric body. During the course of human evolution, the energies of the centers became condensed in a particular location in the physical form. This resulted in the generation of seven major endocrine glands, each of which are associated with the corresponding major etheric centers.

Each of the endocrine glands are conditioned by the quality and type of energy flowing from the etheric center. The following relationship occurs:

| **Etheric Center** | related to | **Endocrine Gland** |
|---|---|---|
| 1. Head center | | Pineal gland |
| 2. Center between eyebrows | | Pituitary and Carotid gland |
| 3. Throat center | | Thyroid and parathyroid gland |
| 4. Heart center | | Thymus gland |
| 5. Solar plexus center | | Pancreas |
| 6. Sacral center | | Gonads |
| 7. Base of spine center | | Adrenal |

When the individual 'reacts' to impulses from the etheric centers, hormones are secreted into the blood stream. This stimulates and influences him with its life forces into the overall physical body-system. The endocrine glands and the etheric centers therefore provide a significant controlling factor in the health of the human body.

**The Spiritual Triad**

The Spiritual Triad is often referred to as the 'Higher Mind' and constitutes the "spiritual man" in incarnation.

Just as the Soul expresses through its 3-Fold personality on the mental, emotional, and physical planes, the Monad expresses itself through higher vibratory substance called the atma, buddhi, and manas.

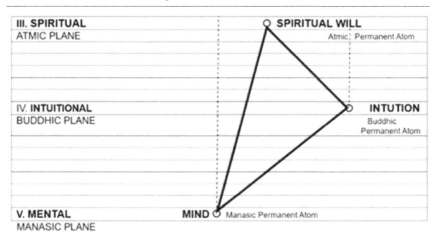

This acts as a guidepost for the Soul, disciples and Initiates for achieving the higher initiations. Each of these permanent atoms correspond to the 3 Aspects and are composed of the following substance:

- Atma – (Spiritual Will) The atmic is the plane and the source of eternal ideas, archetypes, and principles.

- Buddhi – (Spiritual Love / Wisdom) Buddhi is made up of pure love, intuition, pure reason, and is the carrier of (formless) ideas.

- Manas – (Higher mind or Intelligence) Manas means 'mind' and refers to the higher part of the mental plane.

These are life-giving energies transmitted directly from the Monad and available when the disciple is evolved enough to receive them. The Monad transmits these energies via the Soul through what are known as the "life and consciousness threads" to the lower three worlds.

It is important to know that the personality when integrated cannot directly contact the Monad until after the 3rd Initiation has occurred. At that time, the strength of these energies is felt in the Initiate's consciousness for the first time and a significant achievement in the Soul's evolution has occurred. As the Initiate, he can now communicate directly with the Monad.

On the Path of Liberation, the Soul guides the lower personality for *integrating and replacing the lesser expression of matter with the higher correspondence in the Spiritual Triad.* For example buddhi replaces astral matter and manas replaces kama-manas (lower desire). Eventually, the higher substance of these 3 aspects of the higher triad will replace the entire lower trinity.

Beginning with the Probationary Path, the Soul helps the personality in creating a bridge or Antakarana between the abstract mind and the higher manas. This will allow the intuition and pure reason to flow and bring the higher knowledge down to earth.

The atma, buddhi, and manas energies of the Spiritual Triad are the bodies through which the Monad connects and functions with the denser lower planes. From our perspective on the lower planes, those higher energies act like a magnet, which eventually draw spiritual man to exchange the lower mental with the manas; the emotional for the buddhi and embody atma (inculcating the activity aspect) into the physical. The following analogy will help to explain.

If you stand in front of a mirror, you see a version of yourself – the physical form or personality. You will typically equate it with your personality. Although it is a part of you, it is not the true you just as a drop is not the ocean.

If you look deeper as an observer and connect with your higher Self in meditation, you can realize your consciousness is beyond just a physical identification.

The Ageless Wisdom Teachings allow us to look deeper into our own consciousness. Through meditation, we learn that when we connect our personality with the Higher Self or the Soul, we see ourselves as we really are, and can 'become that'. This higher identification makes it possible for the personality to integrate the higher energies of atma, buddhi, and manas, of the Spiritual Triad with the energies of the mental, emotional, and physical bodies of the lower triad. Over time and through meditation, an integration occurs that ultimately enables initiation, where the lesser man "becomes higher Self."

With each successive energy transference between the Spiritual Triad and the lower personality takes place. This results in transformations and expansion of consciousness and furthers the evolution of the lower bodies. When, for example, enough buddhic energy replaces its corresponding lower emotional-astral, then the aspirant will have inculcated the energies of intuition, pure reason and the intelligent application of love into his being.

**Implementing the Higher Transference**
In order for the personality to evolve through the Soul's guidance and make contact with the higher energies of the Spiritual Triad, he must have a considerable amount of Soul-infusion already in his consciousness. Generally speaking, the first three initiations indicate a progressive and increasing amount of Soul-infusion and purification of the etheric body:

- 1st Initiation – 25%

- 2nd Initiation – 50%

- 3rd Initiation – 75%

The Atma, Buddhi, and Manas energies act as a fire and will stimulate the disciple, and later the initiate-to-be in his etheric body, and mind.

This will result in a crisis in the consciousness in the initiates' life that will culminate in an expansion of consciousness. When the initiate achieves, for example the 1st Initiation, he will have infused or replaced 25% of his personality consciousness with that of the energies of the Spiritual Triad, via the Soul.

At that point, the Soul is very much driving the thoughts and actions of the personality.

## Emotional and Mental Planes

> One of the first things then that the aspirant has to learn is to dissociate his own aura in the emotional sense from that of his surroundings and much time is expended in learning to do this. It is for this reason that one of the first qualifications of discipleship is discrimination, for it is through the use of the mind, as analyzer and separator, that the astral body is brought under control.
>
> Alice A Bailey, "A Treatise in White Magic"

➡ Note: The following section describes the basic aspects of the emotional and mental nature, and their purpose. Although both have many characteristics and nuanced interconnections as part of the integration process, these will be discussed in greater detail in the chapter "Building Towards Integration".

### Emotional-Astral body – the Plane of Emotions

A Google definition of "emotions" and "feelings":

> "....A fundamental difference between feelings and emotions is that feelings are experienced consciously, while emotions manifest either consciously or subconsciously".

The emotional-astral plane is a conglomeration of emotions, feelings, and anxieties, which often contribute to illusion or a distorted depiction of reality.

A major purpose of the Path of Liberation is to completely purge all distorted views of reality for enabling clear seeing on all planes of who and what you truly are. This is first achieved through alignment and integration with the Soul.

The esotericist understands that emotion stimulates the mental and "feeling" nature of the emotional-astral body.

By its nature, it either attracts or repels emotions. In this way, aspects and expressions of the personality either become attractive or pushing away, i.e. repulsive. This is demonstrated when fear, love, jealousy, separation, hate, anger, greed, and desire are present as the emotions "react" to someone or something in the environment.

From this, the esotericist is cognizant of the dualities felt in his emotional-astral body, such as feeling pleasure and the opposite pain. At some point on his path, he will understand that becoming unattached through dispassion and bringing balance and alignment with the Soul will result in integration and eventual liberation.

While in meditation, negative emotions are observed in how they create separation in consciousness from others and blocks any higher inspiration from Soul. Through a mental understanding and applied techniques, negative emotions can be transformed.

**Notes on the Emotional-Astral body**

- Impressions can be registered in the astral body or the abstract mind. The disciple must carefully learn to distinguish between emotional responses in the emotional body and impressions from the Soul.

- When a measure of alignment and integration are achieved with the Soul, negative "reactive" emotional energies are replaced with the higher correspondence of buddhi from the Spiritual Triad.

  o Emotions produce feelings of pleasure and pain.
  o The buddhi energy as a finer vibration of matter, represents a higher expression of love, sensitivity, compassion, pure reason, and intuition and causes refinement and redemption of the lower emotional-astral matter.

- When you are confronted with a glamour or illusion in your emotional-astral body, it is best dealt with on the mental plane. Using the Technique of Light (see Appendix A) you can bring focus and awareness to *what* you are emotionally dealing with, by merging your consciousness with the higher light of the Soul.
  - Your task *is not* to get rid of these energies or judge them per se, but acknowledge they are limiting factors in expanding your spiritual awareness.
  - This technique is most effective when the hinderance or obstacle in the emotional-astral body is identified and the personality and Soul work in cooperation to shed light on it to transform it into something more life-giving.
  - Working with this technique, this process has the potential of *"shocking the aspirant or disciple"* into action.
  - In the advanced stages of spiritual development during the 2nd Initiation, the disciple will willfully suppress any feelings that are destructive to the Soul's nature.

**Mental Plane**

The lower mental plane governs your thinking process, discrimination in thought and how you differentiate or organize things in the mind. This lower aspect consists of the Concrete and Desire mind. The higher aspect (at the Soul level) consists of the Abstract Mind, the Son of Mind or the Soul and the Transcendental Mind.

The highest aspect of the Soul and Mental plane is manas. Manas is the lowest part of the Spiritual Triad and the means whereby the Soul connects to the Spiritual Triad. Reference the Spiritual Triad diagram in this chapter.

In the Ageless Wisdom Teachings, the mind of man is made up of five basic parts:

Kama-manas or Desire Mind: is connected with emotion; the desire-mind is deluded by the world of form and seeks to acquire experiences consisting of personal desire, usually resulting in experiencing pain or pleasure.

This is the combination of astral-emotional and lower mental (concrete mind) energy. Together this generates glamour and illusion in the lower 18 subplanes.

Concrete Mind: This is man's main faculty for cognition of his life and environment. It functions as the lowest form of the "thinking" nature. It has the capacity for logical deduction, rationalization, discrimination, reasoning, and discovery. The hallmark of the lower mind is that it knows how to "separate" and identify.

When the personality is integrated, the world of thought is opened up and the lower mind can become an instrument of the abstract mind.

Abstract Mind: functions as a bridge between the lower concrete mind and the highest aspect of the Soul. Together, this bridge connects the lower and higher mental plane with the Spiritual Triad.

The abstract mind is the lowest aspect of the Spiritual Triad and acts as a conduit for conveying illumination, impressions, ideas, intuition, divine love, and pure reason to the lower mind. These energies can be channeled into service-related activities on the physical plane. This type of connection becomes possible when the personality is aligned with the Soul through meditation, and begins to construct the Antakarana on the Probationary path.

The abstract mind is the faculty cultivated by the personality that can comprehend physical plane reality.

Son of Mind: is the Soul (located on the 1st and 2nd subplane of the Mental plane) and who is the thinking and perceiving entity. It is characterized by pure mind, pure love, and pure will.

| V | | (A MIND | Manasic Permanent Atom | Higher Abstract Mind | 1 |
|---|---|---|---|---|---|
| MENTAL | Antahkarana | | △ Soul or Causal Body | | 2 |
| MANASIC PLANE | | | | | 3 |
| COSMIC GASEOUS | | | ♭ Mental Unit | Lower Concrete Mind | 4 |
| | | | | | 5 |
| | | | | | 6 |
| | | | | | 7 |
| VI ASTRAL | | | ♂ Astral Permanent Atom | | |

It is the Soul that redeems the matter and substance of the lower three bodies into a higher planes expression.

The Soul is made up of a causal body and permanent atoms. It is also known as the Solarized Mind or Christ principle, and represents the intelligence principle. As the keeper of wisdom, it communicates to the personality through the light of impression.

The Soul's main purpose is to facilitate the evolution of its lower reflection, the personality, to become like itself.

Through spiritual living and the experiences the personality accumulates over a given lifetime, the Soul stores the highest wisdom and essence learned from both the 'good' and 'bad' experiences in its casual body.

The causal body is the temple of the he Soul (1st and 2nd subplane of the Mental plane). It lasts throughout all incarnations and is only destroyed at the 4th initiation when all karmic experiences are purified and the need for the human to incarnate and continue the cycle of rebirth is no longer necessary.

Esotericists understand that 'bad' actions or karma are the unwise use of energy and force often through selfish motive by the personality. When we speak of karma in this way, we are usually referring to events and situations in a particular lifetime where the personality was focused on expressing motives, which may be selfish and the Soul was not the guiding factor.

In cases like this, there is a stored "negative" energy in the causal body that must be transformed and purified.

'Good' energy is referring to a higher expression of consciousness within the personality produced by performing non-selfish deeds, such as altruism and service to others.

From this, your personality learns the wise use of this knowledge in combination with energy (made up of thoughts, feelings and physical activities) and force together with the Soul, facilitates spiritual growth. This is facilitated by the abstract and rational minds working together as a unit when motivated by the principle of love. The Soul expresses love and abstract intelligence via its light. Employing esoteric meditation, the personality and brain become synchronized together, resulting in illumination in the mind.

➤ Note: The right use of the Soul's intellect is to heal cleavages in the personality. For greater detail on "Cleavage" see chapter Building Towards Integration, subsection Problem of Cleavage.

Transcendental Mind is associated with the consciousness of buddhi or the Plane of the Intuition. The Soul acts as a bridge between the Intuitional Plane and the lower planes of the 3-Fold personality. When the Antakarana is built, the disciple-personality can access this higher mind and bring forth the energies of buddhi and purify the lower bodies. For this process, the lower matter of the astral body is replaced with buddhic substance.

- When enough Soul integration of the lower mind happens through contact with the abstract mind, the will aspect of the Soul begins to govern man's mental nature.
- Manas includes both the lower Concrete mind and the higher mind of the Soul.

# Building Towards Integration

Stages of Soul and Personality Integration

> *As the energy of Divine Will or light impacts the consciousness of a beginner on the path, we see it manifesting within his mind as the Will to Good. This is the first major step he takes in his re-orientation towards embracing the Soul's consciousness.*
>
> Lucille Cedercrans – "The Nature of The Soul"

In the chapter "Human Constitution", we discussed the various "bodies" and parts of the personality. In his chapter we will discussing information about what what takes place during the integration process and how you can take the knowledge and learn to apply it in your life.

There are three main themes:

- Description and definition of the integration process.

- Stages and Transformation of Personality Integration

- Various forms of limitations and obstacles you encounter during the integration process. With the elimination of obstacles (purification), you will be able to transcend anything in consciousness that keeps you from spiritually moving forward with a greater expansion of consciousness.

On the Path of Return, you will learn to integrate the mental, emotional, and physical bodies into a relation whole. You will do this in stages as your consciousness will expand and will attain a more inclusive awareness, wisdom and understanding. When it is united in this way, you will learn to function as one intelligent, loving and living being.

In the initial phases of the integration process, you must realize you are dealing with Soul objectives and not those of the personality. The Soul seeks to infuse and control the lower 3-fold mental, emotional, and physical bodies with the purpose of creating a "whole integrated instrument" and to become sensitive to impressions from this higher reflection.

From the outset, Soul contact is not integration but regular meditation will help make possible a balanced and "integrated personality". When this happens, the light of the personality and the Soul blend and become the "lighted way". The personality must have a clear and definitive "mental understanding" in order to move forward. To facilitate integration, he must first create a firm and stable foundation in his lower concrete mental nature. This establishes a mental perspective and not emotional. As stated in the chapter "Human Constitution", the Self or Soul manifests as:

- Lower intelligent (concrete) mind on the mental plane;

- Abstract mind as the highest aspect of the mental plane.

The abstract mind is the means for the personality to contact the Soul and later the Spiritual Triad. This will allow impressions and buddhi to come forth from the Plane of the Intuition and replace the lower energies of the personality.

This then becomes a Science of Integration whereby the aspirant learns to develop the following in the mind:

- Coordination – of the physical body in relation to the etheric body;

- Alignment – achievement of creating a 3-fold personality;

- Integration – conscious integration of lower mind with the brain and the astral body;

- At-onement of personality with the Soul to create a fusion.

# Stages of Personality Integration

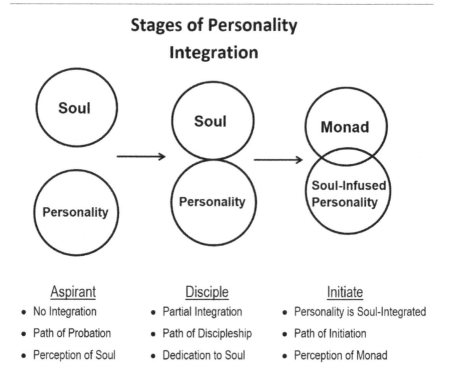

| Aspirant | Disciple | Initiate |
|---|---|---|
| • No Integration | • Partial Integration | • Personality is Soul-Integrated |
| • Path of Probation | • Path of Discipleship | • Path of Initiation |
| • Perception of Soul | • Dedication to Soul | • Perception of Monad |

During this time, you will recognize your relationship and interrelationship with all parts to the whole of your being and how they work together. You will find that dealing with his astral-emotional nature will probably be the most challenging. In your life, purification of your mental and emotional bodies are ongoing. This has allowed the Soul to have a considerable influence over any personality tendencies.

Also understand that emotional and mental changes also effect the physical-etheric form. For this, it necessary to keep in mind the "whole person" and how energies and forces interplay and control. At times, you will find you need to step back, become detached and see the larger picture of integration and personal transformation happening within.

With regular meditation and connecting with the higher mind of the Soul, the gap between the lower bodies will be bridged.

This will bring the personality into a higher awareness and will eventually result in a Soul-integrated personality.

At this point, you have a considerable understanding of the nature of energy (with focused emotions and thoughts) and force (Will) through your practice of meditation and spiritual study. Your life and consciousness and applied livingness demonstrates that you are bringing the Soul's light into your mind with intentionality, while outwardly manifesting this reality as focused service.

At the latter part of the integration process the aspirant will undergo initiations. These are rare events where the consciousness is expanded and the personality is transformed to become more Soul-integrated.

We also see at the level of humanity that it too is progressively learning to integrate all the disparate parts together of the family unit, the social order, the nation, and the world of nations into a relational whole.

Note: There are two central themes discussed in this chapter. One is about personal transformation through various methods and techniques. The other is about purification and overcoming glamour, illusion and maya. Moving from a lesser state of consciousness to a higher one requires you as the aspirant remove all obstacles in consciousness that block the radiant life of the Soul.

➡ In addition to describing the stages of development along the path, various supplemental information related to the integration process are included in the Appendix A "Techniques for Working in Consciousness".

The process of Soul Integration happens through the following stages:

- Path of the Mystic

- Path of Probation

- Path of Discipleship

- Path of Initiation

During these stages, the aspirant will go through numerous expansions of consciousness and purifications of anything that blocks a direct Soul connection.

## Path of the Mystic

The Mystical Path is characterized by devotion to a person or ideal and possibly having a feeling of pure 'beingness.' The Mystic does not necessarily inquire about the experiences in his mind. At this stage, he expresses great love and devotion towards a cause, a teaching, or teacher, quite possibly for many lifetimes.

In the Ageless Wisdom teachings we understand that our primary teacher is the Soul, which guides our inner spiritual development. A true teacher just as a great leader, is somebody you should not follow blindly, but show you qualities and assets you already have. The teacher will encourage you to use your gifts and show you how to nurture them. The true teacher will see your weaknesses, and together, you will work with him or her to realize how to move through any issues. The devotee must be open in his heart and mind to answers. He does this typically through prayer work. Looking for answers to difficult questions and guidance can take some time to resolve.

Eventually a lifetime will come where the mystic will want to expand his consciousness and want to *know about* what he has been so enthralled about beyond the devotional stage. The path of the mystic can be seen as a preparation period for acquiring knowledge. This will draw him onto the Probationary Path.

Nearing the end of the path of the mystic, he will begin to yearn for knowledge about the forces and energies that influence him.

He may have mystical experiences that can cause changes in consciousness. He may ask *"Why is this problem happening"* or *"What is the meaning of this experience?"* or *"How can I achieve or connect to this higher level of consciousness again?"*

This yearning will cause him to be drawn onto the Probationary Path and after a measure of purification, he will take the 1st Initiation.

Note: detailed descriptions of each initiation are described in this chapter under the heading "Crisis Precedes Revelation".

**Path of Probation**

The Probationary path begins when the aspirant leaves the mystical path and has stepped onto the path of evolution. He begins the work of integrating and aligning his lower 3-fold nature on the side of the forces of evolution. At that time, he works at building his own character and brings his personality under control through purification of his physical appetites before reining in his emotional-astral nature, especially reactivity.

The individual begins to ask and inquire about how and why situations happen in his life. This will cause him to begin to study the nature of energy and force, e.g. use of the will as an influence, as he simultaneously purifies his lower bodies by letting go of addictions.

In a broad sense, addiction is the persistent and compulsive activity that is harmful to the user. In the esoteric sense, this refers to behavior(s) that the aspirant knows to be harmful to the spiritual path and connection with the Soul. In this way, addiction can be either material or subjective. Examples of the most common addictions are drinking, drug use, cravings of the flesh, over shopping, and gambling.

Addictions are directly related to glamour (illusions in the astral body), Maya (illusions in the physical form), or illusions in the mind.

Although the aspirant will not have mastered his or her lesser tendencies until he nears the end of the spiritual path, there is nevertheless an ongoing process of purification, which lasts lifetimes. The control and transformation of one's lesser tendencies to a higher and more expansive perspective are central to the aspirant's initial development and growth.

When moving from one stage of consciousness to another, overcoming the emotional-astral nature is considered the most difficult process one will go through and which takes the most time. This is most evident in the probationary stage, where the aspirant is tested by the Soul. To grasp this, one only has to realize how difficult it is to release an emotional attachment to a person or thing. In the latter stages of the path, the aspirant will learn to control his astral-emotional nature through an act of will by mentally knowing how to work with and deal with the energies in his consciousness.

At this stage, he will begin a preliminary spiritual study of Maya (physical cravings), Glamour (emotional-astral), and Illusion (mental) on the Probationary Path. He practices responsibility, goodwill, and cooperation in his life's encounters. He begins to see and understand the importance of bringing harmlessness and selflessness to service-related activities. Through these efforts he works at building his character in the image of the Soul, and employing its higher values. As a result, the Soul's casual body, which stores all previous experiences of previous incarnations is purified and becomes a receptacle for the Christ-principle.

The Christ Principle indicates the illusive but potent energy of the Christ within an individual. This energy is always part of the Soul, and can be accessed by aligning with the Soul and expressing its values, such as goodwill and selfless love.

For one who holds this alignment, he has become a living embodiment of this energy and exhibiting all its qualities. This is in effect an identification with this type of energy, while exhibiting all of its qualities.

The main characteristics of the Christ-principle is selfless love, evoking the spirit of understanding, goodwill and cooperation. For most people, it is expressed as an urge towards bettering human relationships.

The probationary stage can last lifetimes and is highlighted with purification of the mind, thoughts and emotions. During this time, his consciousness is influenced by three major activities in consciousness:

- Increased mental activity: the aspirant must learn to control the mind and stabilize it, so it can be used as an instrument in service at his command.

  At this time, subjective training happens without him consciously knowing it. He is taught by his Soul through impression to learn to know himself on deeper levels, his weaknesses and to correct them. He learns the rudiments and the power that glamour and maya have over his personality. The Soul seeks to lift the aspirant from the emotional-reactive world and into the mind.

  He seeks to establish a modicum of rhythmic living and moving towards self knowledge. He can begin deeper understanding of the lower self and the Soul through spiritual study. He begins the process of recognition of the not-self, or knowing the parts of the lower self that does not express the Soul's light and love.

  From this study, he learns the basic concepts of training himself for service and to analyze his motives.

- Increased responsiveness to ideas: As much as he removes obstacles in consciousness, he grows with increasing sensitivity to the inner voice of the Soul, its urges or impressions. With this, this will cause an inclination towards adapting new ideas and service related activity for the betterment of humanity.

- Increased psychic sensitivity: The aspirant is influenced by allurement of psychic powers and learns not use them for self-gain. His faculty of intuition begins to develop.

**Key points for Transformation**

This path is probationary in the sense of how the Soul might evaluate and guide the person's growth. As much as the probationer clears away blockages and senses energies from the higher planes, his consciousness will expand.

Due to an increasing Soul influence, a probationer might be inclined to take him or herself outside of his comfort zone, and take risks, such as overcoming an addictive habit, or facing a fear in order to grow spiritually. Using the "As If" technique will allow the probationer to emulate a higher Soul energy to move past troublesome energy in consciousness. See Appendix A "Techniques for Working in Consciousness".

This is a path about learning responsibility for one's own actions. Practicing self-control over thoughts, feelings, and actions paves the way towards preparation of greater expansions of consciousness, and service. In the purification phase for the aspirant, he must learn to walk the path and endeavor to cause the least negative or harmful impact on others as possible. For this effort he will learn to open his heart to love.

He begins to realize he is making decisions and observations about the self from a "mental" perspective not the emotional.

Sometime at the end of the path of Probation and beginning of path of Discipleship, the individual will take the 1st Initiation.

## Purification: Removing Hinderances and Obstacles in Consciousness

A major concept to grasp about purification is you are progressing from one state of awareness to a higher one. This is done by overcoming the hindrances present at each stage.

A hindrance can be any action, thought, or feeling that prevents you from directly connecting with the pure nature of your Soul. It can also be an energy, e.g. a glamour, illusion (i.e. set of thoughts) that keeps you from knowing a higher truth, or practicing a virtue.

Examples of Hindrances: Anger, fear, selfishness, attachment, worry, doubt, anxiety, laziness, lack of discipline, boredom, critical attitude, harmfulness, restlessness, carelessness, apathy, ill will, and worry.

Working directly with your own personal obstacles and hinderances is in reality dealing with some of your most overt dark thoughts. On the spiritual path, you must learn to take responsibility and deal with the lower thoughts and feelings that keep you separated from others and from our own Soul. These thoughts and feelings can be either conscious or unconscious.

When dealing with these dark thoughts, it is recommended not to repress your dark side, but learn to transform it. This means that you should stand back in consciousness and learn to see your dark thoughts with dispassion. Using dispassion will take the charge off the thought. Keep in mind that thoughts and desires are nothing more than energy and can be transformed.

Some of the most limiting energies of the dark side that need to be overcome are:

*Anger* poisons the mind and blocks the expression of love from the Soul. This energy must be mastered and contained before moving onto higher levels of consciousness.

The energy of anger, ill will or harmfulness will cripple your service to others, and inhibit your progress on the path.

*Selfishness – Separtiveness* This energy causes the individual to do whatever he sees fit, as he is expressing a 'me only' consciousness.

This can take the form of a passive-aggressive attitude, deception, lying, lack of kindness or compassion; *"I'm in it for me…my family only", my nation or race"*, etc. This blocks out any expression of the Soul, and separates the individual from others.

Addressing this energy is about transforming your own personal will into an expression of the Divine Will.

*Fear – Worry*
Fear and worry happens to all of us, and can even be felt by high level initiates. It has two main expressions:

- It can paralyze you from moving forward.

- Or, it can also be a motivator when courage, in combination with consciously knowing what needs to happen in the moment is present. This can involve an instinctual or strong Soul presence.

In the Ageless Wisdom Teachings, fear and worry are seen as emotions, or energy that are best dealt with from one level above, i.e. from the mental plane.

With these energies, it is recommended to mentally force out the fear by the dynamic power of substitution. You can do this using o the "Technique of Light" or the "As If" technique. See Appendix A "Techniques for Working in Consciousness".

**The Nature of Desire**

Desire is the lowest form of will. As an esotericist, you will want to train yourself to be the observer on the physical plane and learn to differentiate between desire and emotion.

You must learn to become aware of your own inner attitudes and improve how you conduct yourself with others and circumstance of living. You will learn that being "Soul-motivated "will focus you in your day-to-day thinking and activities.

*What is the difference between desires and emotions?* The fundamental differences are:

'Desires' characterize a wanting or grasping feeling. These are astral or emotional feelings stimulated by lesser mental thoughts, which entered the astral body, e.g. *"I want this for my own satisfaction..."* The energy of desire drives man to "overly want" e.g. objects, shopping, gambling, alcohol, drugs, sex, going into debt, sports, or physical exercise. Any of these can lead to obsessions or addictions in the mental or emotional-astral bodies.

'Emotion' is the relationship between thought and feeling. When a person feels and thinks about a feeling, then the reaction is felt in the astral body. This creates emotion.

A significant portion of the emotional-astral nature is made up of kama-manas or desire-mind. It is deluded by the world of form and emotion and causes man to want to acquire experiences usually resulting in experiencing pain or pleasure. The problem of kama-manas or lower desire mind vitalizes or satiates the emotional-astral nature, blocks out the Soul's presence, and can generate glamour and illusion in the lower planes.

Overcoming the Desire Nature

The initial control of the desire nature begins on the Probationary Path and continues well into the paths of Discipleship and Initiation.

Learning to control desire will go a long way towards making spiritual progress. By employing higher desire or aspiration it allows you to connect with the energies of the Soul and integrate the lower personality with buddhi in your consciousness.

When you align with the higher desires of the Soul, your lower emotions and desires become tamed and quiet. To achieve this state, practice the following:

- Acceptance – this is holding a positive attitude regarding the conditions in which you live. Ideally, this will be a right understanding in the concrete mind / personality of life's situations where you the spiritual seeker will not be overcome by lower desire, feelings of '*I don't have what I want,*' or '*I need to be in control.*'

- Poise – Practicing poise involves completely subduing all the emotional reactivity and minimizing emotional disturbances in the personality. Here we contrast "reacting to someone or situation" in favor of "responding". A response comes from a place of poise in awareness and leads to greater discrimination and mental clarity.

- Redemption – The aspirant practices aspiration towards the Soul. Here, you take a mental approach in meditation. In this process, you will consciously redeem or replace the lower emotional-astral nature with the energies of the buddhi from the Plane of the Intuition.

Note, in this work, it is important to reiterate that we are not advocating the turning off or negating the emotions. Rather, to refine the emotional body by allowing the higher expression of buddhi from the Buddhic Plane to transform it.

Purification of the Personality Bodies

One of the most important considerations on the subject of integration with the Soul is about purification of the lower mental, emotional and physical-etheric bodies. It is an ongoing process, especially during the stages of probation, discipleship and initiation.

A large portion of the purification process is about purifying the mind and emotions of any thoughts and feelings that are not of the Soul's nature.

These keep you from experiencing a full integration with the Soul and the higher planes. By purifying your thoughts and the emotional body you are actually making them better receptors for the Soul's light.

In the early stages of purification, the aspirant is unaware a transference of energies is occurring between the Soul and the emotional and lower mental planes. While this is happening he is learning to watch his thoughts, practice harmlessness and lead a virtuous life.

By aligning with the Soul, the aspirant will purify each of these bodies. This will help in the process of integration and provide healthy bodies for the energies of the Soul to flow. With this work, you must purify the lower 3-Fold nature.

When the aspirant learns to dissociate his own aura in the emotional sense from that of his surroundings he will bring the astral body under control. This will go a long way for preparing one's consciousness towards discipleship.


The Plane of Emotions

The emotional-astral body is for most people the most important body or vehicle to transform. It is a conglomeration of emotions, feelings, and anxieties, which often contribute to illusion or a distorted depiction of reality. A major purpose of the Path of Liberation is to completely purge all distorted views of reality for enabling clear seeing on all planes of who and what you truly are. This is first achieved through alignment and integration with the Soul.

The esotericist understands that emotion stimulates the "feeling" nature of the emotional-astral body. By its nature, it either attracts or repels emotions.

This is demonstrated when fear, love, jealousy, separation, hate, anger, greed, and desire are present, the emotions "react" to someone or something in the environment.

His goal should be to make the personality the reflector of higher truths of the Soul and not let reactivity of the solar plexus be your guide. A calm mirror-like solar plexus will then become an accurate reflector of the Soul's aspirations and wishes.

He is cognizant of the dualities felt in his emotional-astral body, such as feeling pleasure and the opposite pain. At some point on his path, he will understand that becoming unattached through dispassion and bringing balance and alignment with the Soul will result in integration and eventual liberation.

In meditation, negative emotions are observed in how they create separation in consciousness from others and blocks any higher inspiration from Soul. Through a mental understanding and applied techniques, negative emotions can be transformed.

Notes on the Emotional-Astral body:

Impressions can be registered in the astral body or the abstract mind. The disciple must carefully learn to distinguish between lower emotional responses and those energies from the Soul. This necessitates the need for right discernment and dispassion.

When a measure of alignment and integration are achieved with the Soul, negative "reactive" emotional energies are replaced with the higher correspondence of buddhi from the Plane of the Intuition.

The energy of buddhi from the Plane of the Intuition represents a greater expression of love, sensitivity, compassion, pure reason, and intuition and causes refinement and redemption of the lower emotional-astral matter.

You may become more sensitive and aware of this process either in working as the Observer with spiritual study – as you observe yourself transforming in consciousness over time.

Using the Technique of Light (see Appendix A), it is most effective when the hinderance or obstacle is identified in the emotional-astral body and the personality and Soul work in cooperation to shed light on it to transform it into something more life-giving. At a minimum, the technique will help to dissipate its influence on your personality.

Working with this technique, this process has the potential of "shocking you the aspirant or disciple" into action.

In the advanced stages of spiritual development, during the 2nd Initiation, the disciple will willfully suppress any feelings that are destructive and inimical to the Soul's nature.

Refining the Emotional Body

The Soul's natural state is calm, clear, and of pure awareness. However, getting to this state is perhaps the greatest challenge for the aspirant.

With the emotional body being a reflector of its environment it receives impressions of every passing whim, fancy and desire.

To align and achieve an integration with the Soul's nature, the work must become a "mental exercise" in negating those energies which are counter to the Soul.

Your aim is to make the solar plexus as a mirror-like reflector of the Soul for registering impressions, motives, and energies from the plane of Intuition, and not the lower personality.

Whatever the aspirant does, his emotions should not drive him through compulsive behavior or coming from a place of reactivity.

Here are some examples of the energies to overcome at the probationary stage:

- Control of over-arching desire, neutralize violent vibrations, fear, worry, discouragement, over-sensitivity to people and opinions, anger, selfishness, attachment, doubt, anxiety, laziness, lack of discipline, boredom, harmfulness, restlessness, carelessness, apathy, and ill will.

- For overactive emotions, it is recommended to practice substitution instead of suppression, for example:

  o Visualization of colors of violet and gold are good for the throat and head centers.

  o Re-patterning thoughts....e.g. negative hate to positive love / inclusiveness, etc.

  o Intoning mantrams can be effective in establishing focus and alignment with the Soul's vibration.

Recommended mantrams? See Appendix A "Techniques for Working in Consciousness"..

Notes on an aligned emotional-astral body:

- The astral body becomes so purified that is reflects the Christ-like principle and the buddhic nature.

- By creating a stable emotional nature, the aspirant develops a sensitivity towards the spirit world and higher consciousness.

- When the astral body is rebuilt with a higher grade substance of aspiration, it becomes a useful vehicle for the buddhic energy to flow through.

- Practicing dispassion and harmlessness allows the consciousness to become a pure reflector of the higher Soul qualities. The mental nature of the Soul can then become dominant and take hold.

In the latter stages of the integration process and in preparation for the 2nd initiation, the aspirant will need to willfully suppress any "reactive emotional tendencies".

Effects of Emotions on the Physical Body

So, what happens when a desire is so strong that you don't get your way, or can't have the object of your desire? Result: the lower mental-body and vital body are impacted or stressed. The medical profession and mainstream media have for a long time recognized a direct correlation between the mind, attitudes, emotions and the body. For example we understand:

Anger centers around an agitated solar plexus (third chakra) located around stomach level.

This can result in problems around digestion, pain in the abdomen, anxiety, fear, worry, bodily tenseness, and headaches.

The nervous and endocrine systems work with the glands. The glands, when stressed will secrete hormones, such as adrenalin into the blood stream causing a general unsettled feeling, possibly fear, anxiety, hatred, separtiveness, and selfishness. With an increased amount of adrenalin in the system, the individual may become more aggressive and unstable. These all block Soul energies.

With feelings of love, goodwill, cooperation, and warmth about your life, your work, and towards people you are with, then the body will not be stressed and works in natural harmony. It can then be a tool for service. This is the spiritual goal we are striving for.

Without emotional stress or lower mental anxiety, the 'higher' mind is engaged. This allows for impressions, higher ideas, ideals, intuition, and flow of Soul's consciousness.

For transforming any of these anxieties, the Technique of Light (see Appendix A) is an excellent tool to overcoming all emotional-astral, Physical - Etheric Body / Vital Body limitations.

**Refining the Mental Body**

An initial challenge for purifying the lower mental nature is eliminating monkey-mind chatter. The mind just as the emotional body must become stable and calm as the Soul's. This will include placing the mind in a listening and observing mode.

This entails:

- Being alert for impressions and telepathic contact. This form of contact can come in the form of imagery or ideas.

- Daily meditation allows the mind to comprehend and gain deeper wisdom, absorb and assimilate higher ideals, such as cooperation, goodwill.

A long-term goal would be to achieve a continuity of consciousness with the Soul so that it's nature permeates all levels of the personality.

When the seeker has progressed a certain distance on the path, then channels for impression and intuition from the Soul open up. This allows for the manifestation of higher values.

With a very quiet mind, you recognize the "Soul's awareness" as a point of tension. You begin to hold that awareness in your conscious waking life.

As the tension is held in meditation, it allows for the livingness aspect of the Soul to freely move within the personality's consciousness.

**Right Thought Building**

One of the basic tenants of spiritual unfoldment is the concept: *"As a Man thinkith in his heart, so is he"*. This aligns with the esoteric axiom: *"energy follows thought"*.

If you stand back, know there are in the spiritual development, two kinds of thoughts:

- Those building towards form-building and limited to physical plane expression.

- Those tending away from the lower 3 planes and leading towards at-onement with the Soul and / or Soul expression.

For thoughts that cultivate astral and physical reactions and results, the aspirant should learn to cultivate the opposite of the inhibiting thoughts. The use of the imagination is encouraged to bring the "higher thought" forth.

By re-patterning those thoughts that do not work, or produce negative results, your mind will learn to control all that it thinks. Shaping your mind in the image of the Soul will create a new intentionality and make all of your life's experiences and activity that of the Soul's purpose.

Character Building

As a probationer you are working in the subtle realms to help offset harmful energies with the opposite energy.

For example, selfishness is replaced with cooperation, goodwill, or harmlessness; aggressive behavior with restraint and tolerance. In your mind, you are learning to identify where in the etheric body the presence of any errant energies.

Character building is ongoing as you are working with a newly acquired sense of responsibility. This is one of the first evidences of Soul contact. You are learning to practice self-control over thoughts, feelings, and actions which pave the way towards preparation for greater expansions of consciousness, and service.

Character Building involves:

- Learning self-control in thought and deed, e.g. overcoming of addictions and taming a reactive nature.

- Becoming aware of forces/energies around you and responsibly working with them by training yourself to become "responsive" and not "reactive".

- Developing sensitivity to the inner world and higher planes, i.e. have a general obedience to impulses from the Soul.

- Beginning to trace the origin of deep anxieties, e.g. fears and anger.

Purification Ongoing

One of the most important considerations on the subject of integration with the Soul is about purification of the lower mental, emotional and physical-etheric bodies.

Purification entails removing anything in consciousness that keeps the individual from realizing the Soul, the higher planes, God, or the Divine. It is an ongoing process that will cover lifetimes.

In the early stages of personal evolution the aspirant begins to purify his thoughts and emotions through contact with the Soul. While unaware of the transference of emotional and thought energies that occur on the inner planes, he must learn to watch his thoughts, practice harmlessness and lead a virtuous life. For the personality, it relates to the purification of the physical, emotional, and mental levels of consciousness.

During the stages of probation, discipleship and initiation, purification is an ongoing and necessary process for the aspirant, the disciple and the initiate. This is an exact science and requires all limitations be overcome in order to progress on the Path.

Purification is about purifying all the bodies:

| | |
|---|---|
| Physical | Dense body |
| Etheric | Internal purity |
| Emotional-Astral | Feeling nature |
| Mental | Concrete mind / mental nature |

For the emotional-astral and the mental bodies, this involves purging any thoughts and feelings that keeps you from experiencing a full integration with the Soul's nature. Purification of these bodies refines and makes them better receptors for the Soul's light.

## Advanced Purification and Transmutation

Transmutation is a process of taking those material energies, either physical or emotional in nature, e.g. the lower energies of anger, hate, selfishness and transforming them into a higher spiritual vibration.

It can also be seen as changing one vibration or vibratory activity into another, or higher one. Since the majority of these forces and energies occur in the astral and dense physical planes, it is the task of the spiritual worker to learn to move these up to the level of the mind where he can deal with them dispassionately. For the aspirant entering the spiritual path, his personality has a relative connection with his Soul as he is still strongly identified with his physical and emotional nature. He is a 'probationer' and developing an obedience to the Soul's impulses.

When he encounters an emotion or selfish thought, he learns to 'transmute' the energy from selfishness into aspiration, and thus making it a life-giving practice. If the energy is desire, he will transmute the desire energy into love and applied service.

# Path of Discipleship

The path of Discipleship or "esotericism" is different from the Mystical and Probationary stages as the disciple is more serious in consciously working in the energies of intelligence and mental awareness of the Soul. In this chapter we will be describing many of the various elements with which the disciple must contend.

For the disciple, there's a near constant need and emphasis for alignment, especially in the early stages for creating a channel of contact between the brain and the subtle planes.

Initially, the 3-Fold personality of the "pre-disciple" is focused in the brain and connected with the objective world. In time, your consciousness gradually expands as you come under the influence of the overshadowing Soul. Through discipline and regular meditation, you will have to familiarize yourself with the new subjective spiritual environment as you deepen your connections with the Soul.

One of the first aspects of clear insight about the changes in your being is understanding the relationship to your mental and emotional nature. This leads to deeper insights into your own nature and provides you some glimpse of the extent of how glamour and illusion have held you and others in thrall.

You will learn to identify areas of cleavage that block Soul energy and will initiate ways to transcend them. This is in preparation for the 2nd Initiation.

Later, when the greater energies of the Spiritual Triad are contacted, you will realize you can attain a fusion with the Soul in consciousness with construction of the Antakarana. With this process, the "conscious" path of discipleship begins. While your subjective life is expanding through deeper alignments, the building of the Antakarana firmly orients you onto the mental plane and de-emphasizes the emotional.

As a disciple, you are ever aware of ebbs and flows of the subjective levels of perception. You come to know and sense the presence of your Soul and its absence.

At times, you will feel empty and seemingly without inner subjective support from the Soul. When this happens, you must rely on your own ability (i.e. knowledge and experience) for bringing forth illumination and knowingness through spiritual study.

With expanded perception, you will find yourself between two worlds or relationship and will act with a "dual consciousness":

- Physical – Emotional….relationship with physical plane life

- Mental – Soul…building orientation towards the Soul

By holding these dualities into close relation, you are establishing the needed synthesis for personality-Soul integration.

Your old point of view is changing and the new understanding is increasingly expanding your spiritual perception of the Soul. You know that the Soul brings greater illumination to the brain, via the mind. This helps you become more confident and effective in your service work. You will learn to consciously register the guidance and support from the Master and his Ashram.

The Hierarchy and Masters as custodians of the Plan are interested in working with disciples who can serve as clear channels of communication to bring forth and concretize subjective ideas into outer material manifestation.

During the intermediate stages of discipleship, you are becoming aware that you belong to or are drawn to be associated to a group of workers at the Ashramic level with whom you should cooperate as a team. This could also be people with whom you are already connected with on the outer planes.

➤ For a description of each of the primary "Stages of Discipleship", see Appendix B.

**Working as an Esotericist**

With the right attitude and orientation, you as the disciple need to strive for keeping an open mind and realize there are no shortcuts to spiritual development and illumination. At times, you will feel extreme fatigue, emotional rebellion, or metal lucidity.

As your consciousness integrates with the Soul, you learn to hold a "don't care" or detached attitude of impersonality towards your emotional-astral tendencies. You are mindful not to allow the emotional nature to react to any pain or distress.

The "difficult" emotions are tolerated, lived through, but not permitted to produce any limitation in your growth. In time, you will learn to live each day as a Soul free from fear or self-consciousness. The astral body is rendered still and quiescent, but sensitive to intuition or impressions from Soul or Master.

In the same vain, you must be ready to release anything that could block new impressions and the revelation of the subjective world. You will find that maintaining a receptive attitude and living in "a state of expectancy", knowing that new visions, ideas and revelations will appear or can prove beneficial.

You must clearly comprehend and carve out every step of the way to expand your awareness and consciousness. Through hard work, intellectual unfoldment, and right spiritual orientation, true discipleship will be earned. At this time you will become an "Accepted disciple" in the eyes of the Ashram and Master. An accepted disciple is one who:

- Accepts the fact of the Hierarchy;

- Is pledged to seek expression as a Soul and invokes the will-to-good;

- Accepts the technique of service;

- Has accepted the Plan and its working out.

At approximately midway on the path of discipleship, the disciple will come to a critical deciding point, which some call "Initiation 2.5". Although the disciple has been seriously working on purifying his emotional and mental nature, there still is astral and lower mental tendencies that need transcending. These are involutionary energies that keeps his consciousness still under the influence of the Dweller. At the same time, he feels an equally strong draw from the Soul, the Ashram and the Master.

By continuing to allow his lower tendencies to dominate him (i.e. the path of Involution), he delays his spiritual progress for any transformations within. Deciding to follow the path of the Soul and move forward on the path of Evolution towards the Ashram and the Master, he will rapidly draw himself towards taking the 3rd Initiation.

After the 3rd initiation, the disciple as Initiate becomes increasingly aware of the synthesis happening in consciousness and his rapid approach to the Ashram where the Christ resides.

Dual Life of the Disciple

For the everyday man, duality is understood as ongoing conflicts in his astral body, such as sensing the difference between light and dark, happy and sad, or pleasure and pain. It appears as a conflict between the Soul and the energies or forces of the lower bodies of the personality.

At this level of awareness, he is mostly unconscious of the dynamics at play. To walk the spiritual path, he must become conscious of the duality in his nature.

On the Path of Probation the awakening aspirant's personality must wrestle with purifying the emotions and its reactive nature. By creating a balance within his own nature, and by bringing in the light or the good, he becomes aware of the dark. From the probationer to disciple, he has been dealing with "dark thoughts", e.g. anger and separatism in his own consciousness.

His next step in purification involves working "mentally" with the concept of duality or the pairs of opposites at the Soul level. He becomes aware that the Soul is turning its attention towards further purifying the mind of the personality. This begins the battle between the Soul and personality.

As a disciple, he learns to see energies and forces, i.e. thoughts, emotions and expression of the will in his life as those that must be harmonized and brought into an equilibrium.

In time, he comes to see how the Soul influences his mental, emotional and physical-etheric bodies. With this ongoing process, his inner spiritual life should be increasingly cultivated. The concept of the "dual life" is about an inner relationship between the personality and the Soul.

Examples of working with duality in consciousness:

- Balancing the male-female interrelationships and energies;
- Learning and knowing what is best for the group (e.g. society, company, family) vs. one's own separative interest;
- Knowing one's own limited and personal will vs. the Divine Will.

As he integrates his consciousness with Soul energies in his daily life, he is also learning to become increasingly aware of subjective energies impinging on his attitude and awareness. This helps him to see the evolution of both his relationship with the Soul and how he relate to others. With his developing awareness, his sense of responsibility is increasing. In his life he is learning true and right proportion in how he conducts himself in service.

He may ask: *Am I taking or giving? Why am I doing this action, making this comment, or what is my relationship with this person?*

The esotericist is one who has dealt with much of the emotional reactivity in his consciousness.

His next step in purification involves working with the concept of duality or the pairs of opposites at the Soul level of the mental plane.

Here, his consciousness becomes a battleground where he stands between the two great forces as the Observer and he realizes his struggle is between his own selfish will, i.e. the personality and that of the Soul and the higher Divine Will. In the end, he will release his own "separative" will and choose the higher Divine Will over all things related to the form and the pulls of the Emotional-astral nature.

Examples of working with duality in consciousness:

- Balancing the Male-Female interrelationships and energies

- Learning and Knowing what is best for the group (society, company, family) vs. one's own selfish interest

- Knowing one's own limited and personal will vs. the Divine Will

A reconciliation of emotional-astral tendencies occurs mostly at the 2nd Initiation where the energies of Buddhi purify the lower emotional and separative energies.

➡ See section "The Final Reckoning of Separation" for a description of this process.

## Working as the Observer

As an esotericist, you are learning to be the observer during meditation. It is strongly recommended for you also to become the observer in your waking life. This activity reveals any hindrances, fears, lower thoughts, etc., and provides the possibility to overcome them. Think of your observing mind as a virus application on a computer, which is constantly scanning the operating system for any malware, or viruses.

It is critical that you know what is in your consciousness at any time, and learn to deal with it.

The great occult injunction says: *Know Thyself!* If you truly look at yourself, then you will become more mindful in the practice of knowing yourself. One meaning of this phrase is when you look at yourself, you want to know yourself in every possible way. You will gain a deeper understanding of your own nature and function of your mind thru the study of becoming the Observer.

*Why is this important?* The subjective realm is the place where all your thoughts and feelings are present and where you can come to an awareness of the Higher Self – the Soul. *What are you observing?*

Initially, you will observe chaotic energies present and need to purify them so you can enable clear seeing. Thru observing the mind you will learn to work consciously with force (expression of the will) and energy. These energies are your thoughts, feelings, and motivations. By going within and observing, you come to know (about) the forces and energies present whether inside or outside of you. Regardless, they are in your consciousness and you must learn to consciously deal with them. During the process of observation, you are learning about your limitations (i.e. hindrances) and your strengths (those that aid you).

Keep in mind that being the Observer never goes away as you can also be "mindful" in your waking state as you are keenly sensitive to all energies present. Sensitivity here is about developing something called the "Esoteric Sense. This is described in the chapter "Setting up a Spiritual Practice – "Spiritual Study."

You will come to know that stilling the mind and the emotions is not enough as you will want to know ABOUT the process of transforming your lower thoughts and practice mental techniques.

Ask:   *How will I do this?*

*What motivates or inspires me?*

Initially, thru spiritual study, you will seek out whatever teachings that inspire or provide insight, and learn methods of purification for expanding awareness.

As much as you align with the Soul, you will observe how your inner nature is changing.

You are focusing and learning on how hold your consciousness, while observing and listening for impressions on the mental plane where the Soul resides.

Other methods for connecting:

- Practicing dispassion and harmlessness, especially when reactive feelings and energies are present.

- Learn to allow the lesser self to withdraw into the background, and let the Soul's awareness and energies flow unimpeded. This will greatly aid in Soul integration.

Over time, the personality gradually becomes transformed in stages during the probationary and discipleship stages.

Stages of the Observer

In esoteric terms, the observer is one who notes where his consciousness is at any moment, particularly in the subjective realms. At first, he will simply be aware of thoughts, feelings, and sensations. Later, as he deepens his connection with the Soul, he will perceive impressions, and phenomena in his field of vision, but he remains unattached.

The observer while in meditation will observe any hindrances entering his consciousness. There he will decide how to deal with the energies present. When in the outer waking consciousness, the intuition can be employed.

Although becoming the Observer and meditating go hand in hand, we will consider becoming the Observer as a necessary first step prior to meditating. The main purpose for becoming the Observer is to guide in the purification process.

We are reminded that activities in consciousness happen over a long periods of time! Becoming the Observer happens in stages, and plays an important role on the Path of Liberation.

There are 3 distinct stages for becoming the Observer.

Stage of Mental Observer

In the initial stages of going within, using a mental focus you observe, as you are peering into the void of your mind.

In this stage the lower mind itself holds the observing awareness. Here you are aware of the contents of your mind, your desires, thoughts, and the forces of your etheric body.

Stage of Pure Awareness

In this stage, the Soul is experienced as awareness. You steadily look within to see what you are and come to the awareness that you are the one who is observing, with pure perception, pure consciousness, and pure seeing. The sense of "I" is strong, and the duality of "self and other" is fully present.

In these first two stages, you realize you have been developing and expanding your consciousness.

State of Non-Duality

In the advanced stage of pure awareness, the 'I' awareness of the personality-Observer, or the one who has been observing disappears all together – as there's just One awareness, that of the Buddhic plane. There we discover our nature is one of radiance, where all creation is experienced as a manifestation and expression of the Higher Self. We see that the Soul is not something located somewhere else or even outside your own nature, but you come to see yourself in all things.

Realize the Divine, by its nature is non-dual, with no separation of any kind. At some point you will have to relinquish your separative "I" nature and completely at-one or merge with the higher consciousness.

This understanding provides a pathway for purification to clear out ALL that blocks you from becoming One with the Divine. This is an unswerving focus upon initiation and upon awakening to the non-dual Reality, and the unfoldment of the naturally existing "divinity" within.

Observing Within

It can be a challenge for the aspirant to mentally or emotionally acknowledge there is a difficult thought, or emotion, e.g. anger, selfishness that needs to be transformed. He can mentally note this energy, but what about over a long period of time?

Perhaps there is a repeating pattern of thought, a powerful feeling, or an impression that comes up? These can be noted in a spiritual diary or journal and/or use mental techniques to transform them.

The journal can be used to note all changes in consciousness that occur around spiritual study, meditation, including your encounters with other people in your daily life.

This style of note taking is important as it helps you understand what is happening in your own mind, allowing you to identify patterns of thought, and recognize the world of the Soul emerging in your consciousness. This form of observation can be particularly useful when practiced over a period of time. This provides a record so you can look back on particular happenings, and study recurring patterns.

For a journal entry, it is suggested that you note the following:

- Impressions, ideas – *Can you trace their origin?* Is the impression or idea clear?

- Significant dreams - note your immediate impressions of the dream and its meaning.

- *Are there any noteworthy symbols?* Symbols can also be a means of Soul contact. What are you leaning from it?

- Note: we acknowledge there are esotericists who do not place much stock in dreams and their meaning. We believe, yes, much of it comes from the subconscious mind, which means that there are lots of potential unresolved emotional-astral issues. Nevertheless, this can be a useful exercise if you are willing to deal with and purify that part of your mind.

- Soul-Urge. The Soul on its own plane will occasionally make contact with the personality. This helps it establish and maintain a 'mental' orientation.

  Over time, the personality learns to develop a capacity for listening to the Soul's impulses, or urges through impressions, dreams and through stimulation of the etheric centers.

In this work, learn to study your own motivations and intentions. For service related activities ask:

*'Am I staying in the moment and motivated by the Soul's awareness of what's needed?'*

Or *'Am I injecting my own understanding of what's needed?'*

Ask often: *What and why am I studying? What am I learning? What is my purpose or intention?*

When engaged in service related activity, are you aware of the Soul's presence? Learn to feel and know what this energy is and to recognize it.

Note any use of the intuition. *Did you pay attention, and implement it? What were the results?*

The esoteric axiom "Inquire the Way" will help to reveal 'who you are,' and 'who you are not.' You the meditator have defined your own meditation practice and will have your own tools for discerning what is right for you.

In the end you must take responsibility for who you are. For after all, you are the builder and knower in consciousness of all that you are. This may sound obvious, but when you experience the depths of your personality, some energies are not so pleasant and must be purified.

In your spiritual journey, you must ultimately confront and purify all parts of your personality and remove all hindrances that keep you from knowing your true Self. Meditation is the most effective means to facilitate integration of the personality with the Soul.

Activities in the Mind as the Observer

Become the Observer (a mental exercise) and separate yourself from the fearful feeling or situation, and willfully relax your physical and emotional-astral bodies.

Perhaps, you can control your breathing, then invoke stillness in the mind thru concentration and permeate the entire personality with pure white light. This is a process of invoking the higher Will for calming your lower mental, emotional, physical bodies.

Complete identification with the pure awareness of the Soul. The more you connect with the Soul or higher awareness through meditation or in outward service activity, the more it will help to displace and replace the lower energies blocking clear seeing and knowing.

Focus on holding higher values in you consciousness, such as love, compassion, cooperation goodwill, harmlessness, a sense of justice, and practiced goodness. These energies will go a long way towards offsetting the lower energies of selfishness, fear, and anger.

Analyze and identify negative energies (whether yours or theirs) – When you feel a negative energy in consciousness, analyze it as the Observer, and try to determine its source. Again, you can invoke the polar opposite to overcome the energy. This is a form of substitution.

## Antakarana Facilitates Soul Integration

For the spiritual seeker, it is not enough to just practice good character, a loving heart and goodwill. When he is beginning to be focused on mental levels, he begins to build the Antakarana.

The Antakarana is Sanskrit for "Inner Organ" or the "Bridge of Light. It is a thread of mental substance that identifies with consciousness and not with form.

The purpose of building the Antakarana is to bridge a "gap" that exists between the lower (Mental Unit) and higher mind (Manas), and the Spiritual Triad. [See diagram on p. 46.]

The gap is a type of break of "unrefined matter" and prevents a free-flow of energies from the higher triad and Soul with the personality.

The Antakarana is made up of the Creative, Consciousness, and Life treads. It is the personality that actively and intelligently builds the creative thread through his life activity.

The "consciousness thread" as it is esoterically known, is anchored in the head and projected by the Soul. The "life thread" or sutratma is anchored in the heart and is withdrawn at the time of death. It provides vitality to the etheric-form nature.

The Antakarana is a symbol of living form. To create it, the aspirant uses the imagination to visualize a line of light. In combination with his projected focused will he creates a connection between the lower concrete mind (as focused mental substance) and the higher manas of the Spiritual Triad. It is a concentrated and focused thought created by the aspirant.

This results in the Antakarana functioning as a bridge or conduit and connecting the Spiritual Triad with the lower 3-Fold personality.

Before this happens, there must exist a a stable connection between the Soul and personality Here, the mind acts as a conduit to guide the process of integration and transference of the atmic, buddhic, and manasic energies from the Spiritual Triad to the personality. This will create a Soul-integrated personality.

During this process, the spiritual seeker understands there are correspondences between the lower 3-Fold personality and the Spiritual Triad. These are:

- The lower mind and thoughts relate to the manas;

- The emotional-astral/emotional relates to the buddhi;

- The physical-etheric relates to the Atma or spiritual Will.

The initial building of the bridge of light or Antakarana begins on the Probationary Path, albeit unconsciously. Sometime in the late probationary or early discipleship paths, the aspirant will begin to consciously build the Antakarana.

To accomplish the first phase of the building process, the aspirant will need to complete a relative measure of purification and removal of cleavages between the personality and the Soul. This would remove any obstacles or hindrance that block this connection.

Over time, the Antakarana is created and is a composite of the following force and energies:

- Force / thought projected and focused by the personality;

- Energy sensed and brought together from the Soul;

- Energy sensed and brought together from the Spiritual Triad.

With a functioning Antakarana, the Soul acting as an intermediary receiving impressions from the Buddhic and atmic planes, transmits them to the lower mind. There, the receptive Soul-integrated personality can interpret the impression and register it in the concrete mind.

When enough of the bridge is built to receive or be open to continual impressions from the Triad, a "continuity of consciousness" will be established. This most likely will happen at the 3rd Initiation.

**Discipleship and the Will**

An initial discussion about will is about whether you are driven by your own freewill or Divine will.

The concept of human freewill requires that you are able to take more than one possible course of action under a given set of circumstances. This can be by thought, physical action, or both.

In society, freewill is closely linked to the concepts of moral responsibility, praise, guilt, sin, and other judgements which apply only to actions that are freely chosen. It is also connected with the concepts of advice, persuasion, deliberation, and prohibition.

Man may be consciously aware of different streams of force in his environment, some of which may be beyond his control. In the world, his freewill has been infringed by authoritative control, dogma, ideology, and corporations who have imposed their will and therefore obstructed personal growth.

When man becomes spiritually awake, he can put himself in a position where he could take advantage of these forces, or not, simply by an act of will with his mind.

This is most often associated with actions of the personality. When the "awake" individual begins to be motivated by a higher vibration, his sense of freewill changes.

He may have freewill within his own local community by sharing his skill or knowledge. The sharing is carried out through his will where it can overlap with others and become an influence. When wills are opposing each other, there are clashes. This requires both opposing parties to consider their own course of action to make their will fulfilled. The effect of the will can also depend on the strength of a single person or a group will united in a common cause. In a worldly context, a person may have a strong personality or someone with vision whom people follow.

There are untold examples of people in history who have expressed their will and influence or played a role in local, state, and international affairs.

Within the Cosmic Physical Plane, the expression of will has different degrees of manifestation. From the plane of the Atma, the will is a full expression of the Monad; from the Buddhic Plane, perfect reason and poise; from the plane of Manas as intelligence.

Often, the personality expresses as selfish freewill and separative consciousness. In one of its most base forms, it can be a manifestation of erotic desire.

In an spiritual context, many people meet and use their wills for meditation and provide influence on the inner planes, such as by using the Great Invocation for meditation for healing. This type of expression constitutes an expression of spiritual force.

In essence, during spiritual development you want to learn and train the mind to use the will in service for the higher purposes of the Soul and not the separated self.

Divine Will

The higher Will coming from Shamballa represents the "Will-to-Good" expressed as divine ideation. Shamballa is known as "the center where the Will of God is known".

As this energy is stepped down by Hierarchy to humanity, it manifests as 3 Aspects: Will / Purpose, Love-Wisdom, and Active Intelligence.

As man spiritually evolves, and his personality is becoming integrated with the Soul, his will power increases. At this time, he learns how the Divine Will works in his consciousness by wielding energy and force through the power of his will.

He can choose to meditate, and control his desire nature for overcoming glamour and illusion by using the Technique of Light, and the As If technique.

The spiritual man does this as he is training to carry out the higher will in service. Therefore, man with his free will chooses personal development.

Hierarchy cannot interfere, but as Guides of the Race They influence man and ultimately humanity through impression.

This enables man to use his Will in accordance with the Divine Will and for positive change.

## Path of Initiation

As the probationer and disciple move on expanding his consciousness, he will simultaneously be drawn towards the path of initiation.

Initiation is a process of penetrating into the mysteries of the science of the Self. The Ageless Wisdom Teachings describe spiritual initiation as a process that centers around crisis, and when successfully completed, it represents a major step in evolution for the personality and the Soul. The Path of Initiation is the final stage of the path of evolution that man takes and is divided into five stages, known as the Five Initiations.

The process involves working directly with energies, forces, and reconciling the pairs of opposites. For this reason the first four initiations must be taken in physical incarnation as they deal with karma and transforming the mental and emotional natures.

Each of the major initiations is considered to be a rare event, and lifetimes can pass between each major shift. A shift represents a paradigm shift in consciousness where the disciple fundamentally transforms an old way of being to the new way of thinking in consciousness.

As much as the initiate clears away blockages and senses energies from the higher planes, he will expand his consciousness. There he demonstrates his ability to comprehend, and work with the knowledge of energy and force as it interacts in his consciousness.

From the Soul's and Master's point of view, the first two initiations are considered to be minor, but it nevertheless represents a milestone for the probationer and disciple in demonstrating control over the lesser astral and mental tendencies.

As much as these tendencies are identified, they are handled from a 'mental' level. This process causes the initiate to become an observer, and knower within his own consciousness.

At the completion of the 2nd Initiation, the disciple is strongly mentally focused and considerably Soul integrated. The initiation process accelerates as the disciple's mind is so attuned to connecting with the higher planes via the Soul.

At this point, the disciple is like a boat drawn by the spiritual currents of the Soul in the direction of the 3rd Initiation. This initiation will culminate in a direct connection with pure Spirit, or Monad that will directly infuse the personalities' consciousness with its pure light to become the dominate force.

The purpose of the 4th Initiation is to completely renounce the personalities' connection with the form nature, i.e. physical incarnation and end the cycle of rebirth. Since all karma has been completely purged, the Soul and causal body are destroyed, thus the cycle of rebirth, and incarnation is no longer necessary.

The 5th Initiation leads the initiate now "Master", into functioning within the greater realms of Higher Evolution.

# Influence of Glamour, Illusion and Maya

In the early stages of the Path, the aspirant must deal with a definite lack of integration of his personality. Spiritual work for this path requires him to shift his polarization from his aspirational–emotional nature towards acquiring a "mental" thinking perspective on resolving problem energies. Sincerity of aspiration is not enough for progressing on the path of integration. You will have to look towards mundane, concrete and spiritual knowledge to give you a sense of the work ahead.

One of the first signs of mental polarization is looking at yourself and making a critical assessment. You must fearlessly face your own nature both subjectively and objectively and begin to look at yourself with impersonality.

When you are working more intelligently, particularly in meditation, you are ploughing your mental field. You will receive occasional intuitive impulses and impressions from the Soul which will evoke action of the mind.

With an honest assessment of your mind (thoughts) and emotions (desires and reactivity) you will see what issues need to be purified in order to deepen a Soul connection. Understanding the nature of glamour, maya and illusion will greatly aid you in Soul integration.

Glamour, Illusion, and Maya

Most of the world's greatest spiritual texts describe illusion in its many forms, as the chief obstacle for the aspirant to overcome. Before he can move on the path of liberation, glamour, illusion, and maya must be confronted and overcome. The individual must deal with them directly in consciousness with help from the Soul. This then becomes a "mental exercise in awareness and understanding".

These are defined as:

Glamour is an illusion in the emotional-astral body, and is associated with emotional limitations in consciousness.

The term kama-manas, or desire-mind describes that which produces glamour in the emotional-astral body. It is overcome by a conscious 'mental' effort by both the personality and the Soul as they shine the higher light of truth and understanding on a particular illusionary thought energy.

Looking at a group or nation, glamour represents the sum total of the desire life, national characteristics, psychological traits the individuals making up the group posses. Any of these energies, such as materialism can feed a dynamic life and constitutes a hold of the group's consciousness on the astral plane. This glamour must be recognized as a fog enveloping humanity. The aspirant who is seeking to dispel world glamour recognizes he is working with energy (thoughts) and that the breaking up of forms must happen. For this work he must use techniques on the mental plane.

Illusion is associated with thought energy where the aspirant sees something in consciousness, but not in its true form. It is these thoughts that become more real than the truth they veil, and consequently control one's approach to interpreting reality. As an esotericist, illusion is the result of not being able to see with clarity on the inner and outer planes. As a result, it blocks the intuition.

The personality in cooperation with the Soul must allow its energies to pour its light through the personality's mind and the brain consciousness.

The majority of the thoughts on the lower mental plane originate from an unfulfilled desire nature and keep the personality stuck on that plane. When lesser ideas and emotions interfere, the mental plane is crowded with intensified illusions.

Thoughts of this nature bar the aspirant from connecting to the Soul, abstract mind and higher subjective realms, i.e. the Buddhic Plane. It is only when the personality makes the effort to connect with buddhi from the Intuitional Plane that the higher light of the intuition will transform and dispel the illusion.

Common illusions to overcome:

The beginning aspirant's nature over emphasizes the feeling nature, particularly from things of the objective-material world or form nature, e.g. glamour of attachment to objects and therefore not of the Soul.

Maya is closely associated with the material / phenomenal world, and matter. As man tries to interpret and understand life and his surroundings, he does not see his thoughts clearly.

Maya is first recognized as a force on the path of probation or purification. The aspirant comes to understand the effects of force in his own life when he becomes the victim of physical force currents in his environment. In time he will see the currents as passing in and out of his etheric body and energy centers.

Associated glamours related to Maya to overcome:

- Materiality: over focus and attraction to material objects or things relating to the world of matter and the form nature.

- Objects and activities acting as a distraction to satiate the desire nature, e.g. sex (indulging the physical nature), over eating, gambling, hedonism, shopping, etc.

The Tibetan Master D.K. also suggests that learning to hold one's mind steady in the light of the Soul will also facilitate clear perception, right outlook and attain a higher mental attitude. This is a mental process and involves directly working in cooperation with the Soul. Here the aspirant must learn to train the mind to function in both the lower worlds and the higher realms with a:

- Cautious spirit

- Decentralization of life from the personality and center on the Soul

- Learn to distinguish between essentials and non-essentials.

- Ask "is this object, emotion, line of thought or activity necessary?" "Is it based on a particular attitude coming from the personality or Soul?"

Overcoming Glamour, Illusion, and Maya

On the Path of Liberation, the personality will often need to overcome the thralldom of glamour, illusion, and maya. This is the action of cleansing both the mental and emotional bodies of any thought or energy that inhibits him from clear seeing and perception of reality. Initially, this can be done by simply taking one's mind off the illusion and thus depriving it of any thought or emotional energy, or attention. For dissipation of maya, focusing on the Soul and its nature will devitalize the lower centers and their activity. This causes the individual to re-focus and express through the higher centers, such as the Throat, Ajna or Crown centers.

Common glamours to overcome:

- Sentimentality: overcoming the desire to love and desire to be loved.

- Devotion: causing one to seek or be devoted to a cause or teacher, a duty or responsibility; related to the desire nature.

➤ To dissipate glamour and illusion, use the "Technique of Light" and "As If technique". See Appendix A

**Problem of Cleavage**

In the course of the human evolutionary process, man has accomplished a series of at-onements. These allowed him to take steps so that their fusion might contribute towards making him a whole person. He could only have done this by being the observer and aware there are divisions or cleavages in his own mental, emotional and etheric nature.

For the aspirant he is confronted with identifying areas in the lower bodies that block Soul integration.

To do this, he also understands he must have guidance from the Soul to aid in removing the cleavages that keep him from knowing the higher Self and mind.

Within the personality, significant cleavages, divisions and separations exist in two basic forms between:

- A particular vehicle that inhibits or blocks fusion and integration;

- The Soul, the Spiritual Triad, and the Divine.

The work of soul-personality integration begins for the aspirant on the probationary path. This process continues through the stages of discipleship and culminates on the path of initiation. Late in the life of the probationer and early life of the disciple, he becomes aware of the effects and separations of his lower nature and realizes it has been in a kind of imprisonment. These separations are known as cleavages.

Cleavages exist either subjectively or in the waking consciousness. It can be found in:

- Dissociation between bodies, e.g. emotional, sentient part of self and mental aspect.

- Making oneself Whole – need to end the cycle of sensed duality.

- Cleavage between man and his outer his environment with the realization of his interconnectedness and interrelationship with environment and the natural world.

- Separation between personality and Soul where the Abstract Mind is not active.

For any existing cleavages, the personality may experience crises and a sense of frustration. Eventually, he learns that the separation is only a temporary condition of consciousness, and it poses the possibility of fulfillment and opportunity. The aspirant or disciple's task is to learn to identify where in the etheric body, the emotional and mental bodies the cleavage lies. Identification can be done during meditation while becoming the Observer.

You will need to develop a mental re-orientation so the personality can re-connect with Soul. With each psychological crises you have, learn to train yourself to bridge any realized cleavages. Successfully bridging is indicative of steps of spiritual progress on the Path.

Mental-Emotional Cleavages

A separation in the emotional and mental bodies inhibits or blocks fusion and integration, such as between and the personality, the Soul and Higher energies. In essence, the aspirant must identify any separations that exist in his consciousness that prevent or inhibit the flow of intuition, impressions and illumination coming from the Soul or Spiritual Triad.

When the aspirant works as the observer in meditation, he works in the "charged" field of energy such as the emotional-astral plane.

There he learns how to allow the forces and energies of the Soul to flow uninhibited throughout the consciousness and the etheric body. For this, he must spiritually "know himself" to see as clearly as the Soul sees, free from the limitation of the lower planes.

He learns that meditating and using the abstract mind facilitates a re-orientation or the personality so it can connect with the Soul, and later with the Spiritual Triad. This is most readily accomplished by bridging the gap between the lower mind and the higher mind. He will bridge this gap by building an Antakarana.

➡ To bridge the gap and build the Antakarana, see section "Antakarana Facilitates Soul Integration in this chapter.

Transforming Cleavage

The best way to identify cleavages is to become sensitive to tensions in one or more bodies. Keep in mind that a cleavage is some type of mental or emotional blockage that keeps you from spiritually moving forward. This can simply be a thought needing to be transformed. Let's look at an example.

You may feel a tension in the lower back. First eliminate the obvious physical cause of the stress. If its been there for some time with no discernable cause, begin to examine your thoughts, feelings, perhaps dreams? Is there an underlying stress causing it?

The cause can be on the etheric level around a particular chakra. Perhaps, its an old re-occurring energy-tension that goes back to your early life. Regardless, acknowledge the tension and become dispassionate about it. See it as just energy that can be transformed by your consciousness. If the tension is something beyond the obvious everyday tensions, use the Technique of Light or to merge your personality consciousness with that of the Soul.

Note, while this section deals specifically with identifying where the cleavage exists in the bodies, to get a fuller understanding of the problem of cleavage, see also the following related topics:

- "Purification – Removing Hinderances and Obstacles in Consciousness

- "Glamour, Illusion and Maya";

- Working as the Observer;
- "Purification of the Personality ".

→ See Appendix A for "Techniques for Working in Consciousness".

Notes on Bridging the Gap in Consciousness

Before an initiation takes place, the aspirant must have begun an initial bridging of the gap in consciousness between the lower and higher minds and higher energies of the Spiritual Triad.

The Atma, Buddhi, and Manas energies of the Spiritual Triad will act as a fire that stimulates the aspirant's etheric and astral bodies, and the mind.

This will result in a crisis in his consciousness that will culminate in an expansion of consciousness.

When the initiate completes the 1st Initiation, he will have infused or replaced approximately 25% of his personality consciousness with that of the energies with the Soul. At that point, the Soul is very much driving the thoughts and actions of the personality.

The 2nd Initiation is a demonstration of a willful control of the emotional-astral body, where up to 50% of the emotional-astral body is purified with buddhi. The 3rd Initiation marks the time when a final blending of the lower mental with the higher manas and the emotional-astral with the buddhi. This blending or fusion allows the initiate to easily bridge the gap in consciousness between the lower mind and the higher.

For the first time, the Initiate's Soul-infused personality has 75% purified matter, and can now come under the direct guidance of the Monad.

The individual learns he is not his body, nor his emotions or thoughts, but that his inner self is the director of thought substance.

These progressive developments create a realization in consciousness that he is the comprehending entity of reality. This strengthens the thought of the Antakarana;

Learn to see and study abstract things and identify with 'reality.' This involves making associations between abstract and concrete ideas or thoughts, and seeing the relationship between them. This can be done through spiritual study;

Meditation allows him to comprehend and gain deeper wisdom and Soul integration. Constant effort to draw forth the intuition by willing your Soul-integrated personality to connect with the Spiritual Triad.

**The Soul-Integrated Personality**

The process of Soul integration occurs by expanding consciousness and attaining, stage by stage an ever more inclusive awareness.

Through a sustained esoteric meditation and connecting with the higher mind of the Soul, the gap between the lower bodies and the higher mind of the Soul will be bridged. This brings your personality into a higher awareness and will result in a Soul-integrated personality.

With this integration, you have an understanding of the nature of energy (focused emotions and thoughts) and force (Will) through your practice of meditation, and spiritual study. Your life and consciousness through meditation and applied livingness, demonstrates that you are bringing the Soul's light into his mind with intentionality, while outwardly manifesting this reality as focused service.

In your practice, you have undergone considerable purification, and allowed the Soul to have a considerable influence over his personality tendencies.

At the latter part of this phase, you will undergo initiations. These are basically expansions of consciousness where the personality is transformed to become more fused and soul-integrated.

The dense physical form is made up of the physical body, its organs, the endocrine system, and the 5 senses.

The etheric / vital body is made up of the chakras, sushumna and the nadis. These are animated by the Soul, via the sutratma and functions on the physical plane through the personality.

On the subtle level, the "etheric" or vital body, is lowest form of response apparatus and represents the focus for Pure Spirit, via the Soul in the dense material world.

The etheric body is directly related to physical health and is seen as the vitalizing energy for the individual while in physical incarnation. Its made up of a more subtle matter than the dense physical form.

Its primary function is to receive and transmit force(s), such as prana and stimulation from the Soul to the organs, endocrine and nervous systems, and the blood stream.

The Splenic center of the etheric body is a transmitter of vital energies that reach the physical form from the sun, prana or other vital forces in the environment.

➡ Note, for other sources of vitality, the Soul animates the vital body through the Life Thread or Sutratma, which conveys the life principle in the Heart and throughout the body, via the blood stream.

The aspirant who is consciously on a spiritual path knows the importance of maintaining the physical-etheric form so it can function as a healthy vehicle for the service of the Soul. The body is composed of "unprepared" lower and dense matter and therefore it is not possible for the higher vibration of the Soul's light to permeate the etheric body in order to have an impact.

Purification of the physical form can come in the form of a eating a healthy diet, exercising, getting a massage to remove toxins, or even enjoying the pure prana from a walk in nature. Its also about holding the mindset that to maintain physical health, its important to seeing a doctor for regular checkups and attend to physical problems that come up.

On the etheric level, purification is about allowing the higher vibration of the Soul to prepare the subtle energies of the etheric form, such as the chakras to be nurtured and vitalized.

**Measuring Spiritual Progress**

A measure of spiritual progress can be made by looking at yourself and observing environmental conditions, and note whether people and events produce any form of "reactivity" within you.

When you observe a contentious news broadcast, a dispute between office workers, or difficulty with a personal relation, you note the whole expression of your nature is involved and process and the event. Note how you feel, think and act, or *not act.*

As you deepen your connection with the Soul, self-knowledge becomes progressive. It reveals your own motives and needs. As time passes, you recognize and trust your higher inclinations or your inmost self.

You see that through understanding and by examining events or objects from the angle of appearances; lower reactivity no longer applies.

In an effort to derive a deeper meaning as expressed through these forms and phenomena, your life will become more full, rich and interesting. As a conscious disciple and esotericist at this stage of awareness, you will learn to watch yourself closely in relation to others.

You will see that certain activities and lines of thought or emotions produce cause and effects in life. As an esotericist, you see these as energies and forces at play.

With this knowledge, you will deepen your sense of responsibility for your own life and learn to "respond" to life's opportunities and not react. Before acting, you will weigh the consequences of your action and motivations, and determine whether these are harmful or not? Will your personality be motivated by impulses of love, and goodwill by the Soul? In your meditations and as the Observer, you will more and more come from the center where life is controlled by the in-dwelling Soul and not a personality motivated by materialistic values and purpose.

**Influence of the Seven Rays**

From Alice A. Bailey's book, Esoteric Psychology, Vol. I., the seven rays can be described as:

> "....the sum total of the Divine Consciousness, of the Universal Mind; They might be regarded as seven intelligent Entities through Whom the plan is working out. They embody divine purpose, express the qualities required for the materializing of that purpose, and They create the forms and are the forms through which the divine idea can be carried forward to completion".....*"A Ray is but a name for a particular force or type of energy, with the emphasis upon the quality which the force exhibits, and not upon the form aspect which it creates."*

Also called the Seven Great Beings or Seven Rishis, they emanate from the Great Bear constellation. The 7 Rays demonstrate 7 types and qualities of force of the ONE or the Absolute.

Each of these rays have their own specific properties and attributes, and has a sevenfold effect on all forms, from the individual, to the group, and eventually all kingdoms.

The rays condition man and the form, in combination with the influence of the Hierarchy and the Plan. It should be borne in mind that the Solar Logos embodies the great cosmic 2nd Ray of Love and Wisdom that is the main guiding force underlying all manifestation in our solar system. Thus, the 2nd Ray determines both the quality and purpose for every expression of life and form.

The Seven Rays are divided into the three Rays of Aspect and the four Rays of Attribute with the following classifications:

Rays of Aspect

1. The Ray of Will, or Power.

2. The Ray of Love-Wisdom.

3. The Ray of Activity or Adaptability.

Rays of Attribute

4. The Ray of Harmony, Beauty, Art, or Unity.

5. The Ray of Concrete Knowledge or Science.

6. The Ray of Abstract Idealism or Devotion.

7. The Ray of Order, Ceremonial Magic, or Law.

Characteristics of the Rays

Each ray is characterized by positive strengths and negative qualities (glamours) and will depend on how the individual expresses his own free will as a predominating energy.

As these rays radiate their energies, they produce changes, disturbances, and impacts on all living beings within the solar system. The rays give meaning to the form world and provide the urge to evolve.

Each phenomenal form is a conscious expression of the Seven Ray Lives and the Plan through its life, quality, appearance, spirit, and soul. As the nature of these seven Lives is consciousness, they work cooperatively and in harmony for the manifestation of the Plan.

Each of the seven Ashrams is overseen by a Master or Ray Lord. As a focus of divine intention, they focus the quality and the will-purpose aspect of a certain ray consciousness.

For the consciousness and life experience of the human being, his personality, Soul, and his mental, emotional, physical/etheric bodies, are all conditioned by a specific ray. Our solar system is a 2nd Ray solar system represented by love-wisdom. It is part of a larger group of 6 other solar systems, each with a different ray type.

To determine your own ray structure and makeup, you must consider how the rays influence the:

- Soul ray

- Personality ray

- Ray of Mental body

- Ray of Astral / Emotional body

- Ray of Physical / Etheric body

A more extensive understanding can also be obtained through a study of the weaknesses (i.e. the glamours) and virtues or strengths for each ray. A list of glamours, attributes and strengths for each ray are listed in Appendix C.

The intention of this book is to study and engage the integration process with the Soul. It is worthwhile to be aware of the rays are as they constitute an important physical, spiritual and esoteric influence in the evolutionary process in the disciple's life and his personal transformation. Suffice it to say, knowing your personality and Soul Ray is important for understanding your own tendencies and motivations in how your personality approaches life's challenges.

➡ Note, the study of the 7 Rays can literally fill volumes and a full discussion is beyond the scope of this book. For a deeper study on the rays and their effects on man, refer to the references in the bibliography.

## Discipleship and the Ashram

There are seven main Ashrams, one for each of the 7 Rays. Disciples all work and serve under the specific influence of one of these Ashrams, which constitutes one Great Ashram. The Christ oversees the entire life of the Great Ashram, which is dedicated to the working out of the Plan. It is the work of the Ashram to act as a vehicle for bringing creativity, philosophical understanding and conceptual thinking into the world.

At its core, each Ashram is a field of unified awareness and spiritual center where the Master gathers his disciples, provides instruction, and feedback. In that Unity there is no "my soul and thy soul" – only the single group life. The group life so dominates the consciousness that there is no expression of the lesser nature, separatism, self-consciousness, personality reactions, or anything of a material nature that ever reaches the Ashram.

The love shared with group members is deep and impersonal and their preoccupation is upon inward unity and not upon any outer activity.

It functions as a magnetic center or point of tension where the fusion of energies, emanating from the Master are directed outward towards a field of service in fulfilling the Plan.

The Master works with the group to focus a particular energy for carrying out the Plan using telepathy, impression, or the intuition.

Disciples can be part of the Master's Group, but are pledged to work under the inspiration of their Soul as it dictates, and directs.

A spiritual worker becomes part of an Ashram when beginning the Probationary Path, albeit he is unconscious of this fact.

The disciple is not considered trusted in the eyes of the Ashram until he attained a measure of purification of his personality and has become harmless. Only disciples with purity of intention and impulse from the Soul, can evoke and contribute to the life of the Ashram.

It is the Soul that guides and develops the disciple in the integration process and prepares him for candidacy to the Ashram. After the disciple redeems and purifies his lower nature sufficiently, he will experience a measure of illumination in his spiritual work, via Soul impulse and intuitive perception. This mental orientation will enable him to effectively work in outer plane groups and help in manifesting the Plan.

Later, after the 1st Initiation, the group's sensitivity allows the disciple to be closer to the heart of the group. After approximately the 2nd Initiation, the disciple is "Accepted" into the group center and can participate in consciously manifesting the Plan subjectively with the Master and group members.

➡ Note, refer also to Appendix B, "Stages of Discipleship".

Intuition and Synthesis

With a measure of integration achieved in the personality's lower 3-Fold nature, he connects with the Soul and learns to consciously blend the pairs of opposites in the Abstract mind of the Soul. This brings forth knowledge and the buddhi energy from the Plane of the Intuition, resulting in a synthesis in consciousness.

By connecting to the Plane of the Intuition, the energy of buddhi streams forth and transforms the lower mental and astral bodies. He experiences non-duality, pure beingness, and pure love.

The advanced disciple or initiate still senses duality from the lower planes through his attraction to matter and form, i.e. being in incarnation and recognizes the pulls of both. He eventually learns to stand between the two great forces in consciousness.

With the duality still present in his mind, he realizes his struggle is between his own lesser will and that of the higher Divine Will. He chooses to stand in spiritual being and treads the middle path.

He realizes his consciousness has been a battleground, where he has stood between the two great forces as the Observer and he realizes his struggle is between his own selfish will, i.e. the personality and that of the Soul and the higher Divine Will. In the end, he will release his own "separative" will and choose the higher Divine Will over all things related to the form and the pulls of the emotional-astral nature.

On the Path of Initiation, there is a blending or reconciliation of the pairs of opposites and is accelerated by the disciple's contact with the buddhi energy. During the 2nd Initiation they are largely reconciled when the lower emotional vehicle is being purified and transformed by the buddhi energy.

Finally, after the third initiation, the energies of the "Dweller on the Threshold" and the Angel of the Presence become dominant in his consciousness. There he is drawn into bringing balance between the Angel, the Dweller and in the integrated personality to end the duality. The final result is that an at-one-ment takes place.

Note, the primary means through which the disciple deals with duality in consciousness is best done through meditation. There he works as the Observer and becomes aware of energies from the Soul bringing balance to his personality bodies.

He learns to strive in bringing forth into his waking life that what he experiences in meditation.

## Soul and Appropriation of Bodies

A subtle point that is implied but often not directly addressed is about your willingness and cooperation to work with the higher Self, the Soul.

You may have faith and perhaps a strong devotion to your spiritual practice and personal transformation, but for the work described devotion is not enough. The Soul wants us to at-one with it so we can function as a fully conscious entity with all the love, the will and the intelligence that it garners.   For this work, we are emphasizing the need to be fully conscious, as much as possible, on all levels when working with the Soul's energy.

At a certain point in personality development the Soul exerts a growing influence over the developing individual personality consciousness. Its energy impacts the personality to bring about a fusion of three major forces, and allows it to enter into realms of consciousness more inclusive and universal in nature. This process, taking place over many lifetimes is called "appropriation of the bodies".

The Soul made the first appropriation at the stage of human evolution known as *individualization*. At that time, the form nature and vehicle were impacted or appropriated by the Soul.

Over untold lifetimes, the personality and form nature went through a gradual development and unfoldment through life experience. During that period the Soul tightened its hold upon its instrument, the lower form nature.

At the second stage, the Tibetan Master D.K. describes the "Approach of Acquiescence". When the aspirant's emotional vehicle is impacted by outside forces of opposition this creates an emotional quandary that he is forced to reconcile. During this stage it is the urgency of the need or desperation which causes asking personality of the man to acquiesce to a higher influence of the Soul. The Soul responds with light and wisdom through impression.

In this example, the Soul is responding to the forces of the lower nature, focused, combined and integrated within the personality.

With regards to appropriation, you are considering the attitude and response of the Soul to the personality and not about the personality's needs imposed on the Soul.

At this stage, it is the Soul's intent to stimulate and awaken the relationship which exists between the personality and the Soul. On a parallel track, this is a similar task for which all people of service are primarily occupied.

Their work is also to facilitate the entrance of Soul energy into the world, by expressing itself through love, goodwill, and creating planetary peace.

The third stage is called the "Touch of Enlightenment". It is about the impact of the disciple and the Soul during the time of initiation. This influence from the Soul effects the mind. Here the forces of the purified personality come together on the mental plane with those of the "approaching" Soul. This helps the disciple through the portals of initiation. This energy has the same effect upon disciples of the world who also are learning to transform their aspiration into the light of initiation.

# Crisis Precedes Revelation

## Embracing Crisis

Someone once said: *'If you don't have a crisis in your life – find one!'* On the face of it, this sounds pretty bizarre, and even counter-intuitive as we typically want to *find peace in our lives and not crisis.* For the esotericist, he does not go looking for a crisis, but he attracts it to himself as he knows it is part of life. *Why?*

He understands the dynamics of it as being an opportunity and the potential of acquiring a greater wisdom as he moves through it.

In the world, crises typically happen around events related to financial, political, environmental, climate, social, personal, e.g. addiction, health, violence, or loss. From an esoteric perspective, we observe that whenever it occurs in either the objective (physical plane) and at the subjective (inner planes) or both, it is usually personality induced resulting from a physical and emotional conflict.

Regardless of the origin, the esotericist knows it is something he must overcome and transform within himself.

*What is being transformed?* It is most likely a certain deep-seated underlying thought pattern in consciousness that blocks him from clear seeing and from direct knowing of how to resolve it. From this process, the esotericist knows two things. He can either stay where he is at in consciousness and not progress. Or, in order to move through the crisis he will then have to purge and transform anything, i.e. glamours, illusions and hinderances that keeps him from *directly knowing* the higher mind, the Soul, or Divinity in his own nature.

The esotericist sees crisis as an energy, i.e. the combination of a thought, feeling, and tension that impacts the lower mental, emotional and physical bodies. This tension provokes him to connect with the Soul and transform it by employing the energies of Will, Love and Intelligence. He may feel stress, tension, and even fear.

In order to expand and bring balance to his consciousness on the lower 18 subplanes, he will have to willfully take the energy, and overcome the obstacles.

With these energies from the Soul, he can invoke clear thinking to meet the crisis and create a new intentionality or clarity in his vision to influence the outcome.

By acting as a conscious agent of cause and effect, he can establish a new energy pattern to follow and contribute towards expanding his awareness.

To do this, he must allow his astral-emotional and mental bodies to become sensitized towards higher impression, new vision, and ideas leading the way forward. When he has successfully done this, he will have dissipated and transformed its power into something more life-giving and his consciousness will expand.

For him, crisis is an opportunity to work as the observer and knower as he transforms his inner self to become the Self.

Through time, experience and understanding, he sees the world as interactions of *energy and force*. With his knowledge, he learns that initiation is another word for evolution of the lesser self achieving deeper integration with the Soul.

Here is a brief description of dynamics of moving through Crisis – Methods of Engagement:

1. Awareness: identify hindrances, thoughts and tensions that block a successful outcome.
   a. Ask: *How well am I aligned with the Soul for invoking love, will and intelligence to effect an outcome?*
2. Visualization: dispassionately see the energies and tensions as cause and effect. See a successful outcome rather than that of the limited personality.

3. Vitalization: To resolve crisis, alignment with Soul and personality allow both head, i.e. new thought and vision to come forth, and the will to take steps and move forward.

   a. Tune into a resolved idea as a "potential" or "present waiting event" from a field of possibilities, to be seen and chosen.

## Path of Initiation

At times during the Integration phase, the aspirant will undergo many expansions of consciousness with greater acquired wisdom. When his consciousness is expanded and his personality is fundamentally transformed to become more fused and Soul-integrated this is a rare event and is called initiation.

Typically, these will happen or overlap during the stages of development and around crisis. Included are brief descriptions of the first three initiations.

First Initiation

Nearing the end of the path of the Mystic, the aspirant will begin to yearn for knowledge about the forces and energies that influence him.

This will draw him onto the Probationary Path. During this time, he is confronted with demonstrating control of the basic physical cravings and appetites, such as from addictions, physical cravings of food, drugs, and sex, and an orientation away from material things, as they run counter to integration with the Soul. These tendencies are related to emotional and lower mental desires felt in the astral body.

With a reorientation towards living a spiritual life and away from the material, he realizes there's more to life than attraction to things on the physical plane. With a new found aspiration, he will deepen his commitment to the Soul and embark on a more serious path of purification of the mental, emotional and physical bodies.

Also at this time, the aspirant is developing a concern for human welfare and begins practicing goodwill and service-related activity. He is now learning to incorporate the newly contacted energies in daily living. With a strong control of these energies, he will have completed the 1st Initiation.

The 1st Initiation is known as the "Birth of the Christ in the Cave of the Heart". The characteristics of the 1st Initiation are:

- Purification, ridding oneself of addictions and selfish behavior, and allowing the Christ-principle to flow in consciousness.

- With these energies firmly in place, it will culminate with 25% Soul infusion in the aspirant's consciousness and etheric body.

A spiritual worker becomes part of a Master's Ashram when beginning the Probationary Path. However, he is not considered *trusted* in the eyes of the Ashram until he attains a measure of purification in his personality and has become harmless. Later, after the 1st Initiation, when he becomes an "Accepted disciple", the group's sensitivity allows the aspirant to be closer to the heart of the group.

Between the 1st and 2nd Initiations, a higher connection with the Soul occurs with a fusion of manas and buddhi, and the beginning of the  construction of the Antakarana. This fusion will allow the Higher Spiritual Will to flow and manifest in consciousness.

It will eventually result in initiation. The Path of Discipleship or Esotericism will begin during this time. It is characterized by a shift from an emotionally focused polarity in the astral body of the personality to a mental focus.

Second Initiation

The 2nd Initiation called *the Baptism*, is generally said to be the most difficult to accomplish and will most likely take more than one lifetime to achieve.

At this initiation, the disciple must <u>demonstrate a firm control</u> of his mental, emotional, and physical personality bodies. The most significant activity involves learning to control the emotional vehicle. The disciple must learn to willfully calm the emotions and bring forth higher aspiration and the energy of love.

This will be done through the mental plane, where the fiery nature of the Soul brings forth the energies of buddhi from the Plane of the Intuition. This process will replace the watery nature of the emotions and help to neutralize, transform and redeem all reactivity and lower desire of the emotional nature.

This does not necessarily mean to suppress all emotions, rather those lower desires and urges which are destructive to the Soul's nature, such as anger, hate, intolerance, separatism, or lower sexual drives. It is the energies of love, joy and beauty that become part of the disciple's life and consciousness. Here, he is bringing all emotions and thoughts in line with the Soul's intent.

This initiation as others are actually a process rather than an event. Within the disciple's mind, it has expanded and he goes forth with a new perspective and awakened senses.

The Tibetan Master D.K. enumerates 6 distinct stages of Discipleship, or levels of attainment that culminate in expansions of consciousness. These facilitate the disciple's spiritual growth.

➡ See Appendix B for a detailed description of each stage of discipleship.

At this time, the disciple will allow the Soul to have complete domination over the emotional-astral body as the energies of the Spiritual Triad begin to be strongly felt. The illumined mind will observe and willfully transmute those lower emotions, glamours, and illusions into aspiration and love.

Only the energies of the Divine life remain. For the disciple, this results in a spiritual conditioning and readjustment on the astral plane to bring his consciousness in line with the Divine Will.

With the lower nature and its urges rapidly dying, the Soul can use the astral body for its own higher purposes, such as service.

The throat center becomes activated as the aspirant is motivated towards creative service.

By quelling the lower emotions and desire, the conscious disciple is learning about duality, difference between right and wrong and right use of energy and force. The emotional-astral 'reactive' energy is being replaced with dispassion and the Buddhic energies of the Spiritual Triad. The disciple-initiate is learning to invoke *pure reason* from the Plane of the Intuition. This will serve as a guidepost in all that he does and thinks.

Over the course of the 2<sup>nd</sup> Initiation, the disciple has developed a strong desire and impulse to serve humanity. He is accepted into the Ashram group center and can participate in consciously manifesting the Plan subjectively with the Master and other group members.

He understands that as much as he is drawn to serve, the capacity for grounding and expressing love can also have the affect of accelerating spiritual progress.

Characteristics of the 2<sup>nd</sup> Initiation:

- All reactivity of the emotional vehicle is completely stilled as it is purified by buddhi from the Plane of the Intuition. It then becomes a pure receptacle for the Soul's energy and service.
- The disciple's mind is driven by being responsive and not reactive, to the energies of buddhi. This allows him to be free from the thralldom of ideas, which cause man to be dominated by desires resulting in rash actions on the physical plane.
- His capacity for criticism and separatism is completely neutralized as he sees all human beings brothers and sisters.
- He intensifies his spiritual devotion to serve humanity.

- Although the disciple possesses a strong desire and impulse to achieve personal progress on the path, he is careful not to harm others through selfishness.

With the completion of the $2^{nd}$ Initiation, the disciple is strongly mentally focused and Soul integrated. Approximately 50% of atomic subplane matter of the personality's etheric body and the lower three bodies has been purified.

The initiation process accelerates as the disciple's mind is so attuned to connecting with the higher planes and the Spiritual Triad, via the Soul.

At approximately midway through the $2^{nd}$ Initiation, the disciple becomes aware of a dynamic in consciousness and must make a decision to respond and resonate to the higher spiritual tension.

It is sensed through the pull of the sutratma (i.e. the life thread) emanating from the Master or from the pull of the Monad. The awareness of this tension represents a major turning point in the consciousness of the disciple.

*Will he continue to be controlled by the lower separative and selfish will, which is the path of Involution or choose the Path of Divine Will and the higher path of Evolution?*

The disciple will not pass to the next stage of discipleship or the $3^{rd}$ Initiation until it is resolved.

- He is challenged to transcend the "path of least resistance" and the pull of the selfish will.
- For him, the draw of the Ashram is powerful, but the disciple can still choose the path of selfishness.

Making the decision to follow the Divine Will, the disciple will feel like he is a boat drawn by a spiritual currents in the direction of the Monad for taking the $3^{rd}$ Initiation.

Third Initiation

Between the 2$^{nd}$ and 3$^{rd}$ Initiations, spiritual evolution is sped up. The disciple has stabilized his emotional-astral nature, and now his focus shifts from the emotional plane to the mental plane.

To inculcate the discipline and concentration necessary as preparation for taking the Third Initiation, he must demonstrate firm control of his mental, emotional, and physical personality bodies.

A mental focus allows the disciple to use the intuition as a tool for sensing relationships, such as with the group, his connection to the higher realms, and how well his lower personality bodies are integrated with the Soul. Thus, the mind of the 'little self,' or concrete mind is decentralized into a broader realm of spiritual being.

The Soul, under the direct guidance of the Monad now has complete control over the mental, emotional, and physical bodies of the Personality.

The Third Initiation is called the *Transfiguration* as the personality has been completely immersed in the radiance of the Monad. At this initiation, about 75% of atomic subplane matter of the personality's etheric body and the lower three bodies has been purified.

This is the first conscious contact with the Monad and represents a milestone in spiritual transformation and initiation.

Characteristics of the 3$^{rd}$ Initiation:

- The initiate is no longer controlled from the emotional plane. He now firmly acts from the mental plane and the impulses of the Monad.
- Through a transfiguration in consciousness, the energies of the abstract mind, the spiritual intuition, and the higher

will are blended together into a living *whole*. The Soul, the personality, and Monad are *One* for the first time.

- The etheric body is now responsive to all thought activity of the mind.
- The emotional vehicle acts as a great reflector of love, intuition, and pure reason from the Buddhic Plane.
- The mental vehicle operates freely through the intuition and perceives reality, not illusion, as inner vision is awakened. The concept of brotherhood / sisterhood is sensed and he knows that there is no separation with *my Soul* and *your Soul*. All Souls are seen as the One Soul, or one great unity. The concept of separtiveness is fully removed from consciousness.

- This integration allows the Initiate to make direct contact with the Monad. The mental vehicle is for the first time responsive to the Monadic Will, and by extension to the Planetary Logos.

- The Initiate has his first glimpse of the Plan, his inner spiritual group, the Planetary Life, and its activities are sensed for the first time.

- The Personality now 'Monad-infused' dominates all personality activity. The Soul fades in influence.

## The Need for Poise and Inner Calm

Inner calm is the result of the dissipation of anything that causes emotional-astral disturbances, such as anger, fear, worry, emotional upheavals, and anything of the not-self.

The aspirant will experience an inner calm through meditation by centering his consciousness in the Soul and by bringing forth the illuminating light of the intuition.

Inner calm is more than just being mentally, emotionally, and spiritually at peace. It infers a state of being where the aspirant has developed enough knowledge and understanding to keep himself spiritual aligned in the face of discord, or stress.

His inner calm is known and felt, his inner self will be marked with poise by balance or equilibrium. He has the ability to be the detached observer and able to resolve emotional states, actions and reactions. This aids in integrating the emotional and mental states. It is from this understanding that the emotional nature and its reactions can only be contained by developing the mental body as the "thinker" and not the "feeler".

*Perfect Poise* indicates complete control of the emotional-astral body, so that emotional upheavals or reactivity are overcome, or at least are greatly minimized in the life of the aspirant.

It indicates an ability to function freely on buddhic levels, owing to complete liberation from all the influences and impulses which are motived from the lower three worlds.

## The Final Reckoning of Separation

During the purification process and from the light of illumination from the Soul, thoughts that are not of the Soul are brought to the surface which depict the lower life in the personality. In the intermediate to advanced stages of the integration process for the disciple, the Dweller on the Threshold begins to exert control over the personality.

It vitalizes everything in the lower nature that exists as astral and mental force that keeps the disciple anchored on the lower planes. In other words, it is a thought representing all unfinished business, unresolved problems, undeclared desires, lower potencies, which has dominated and controlled the personality life for untold lifetimes.

On the path of probation the aspirant may be aware of the influence of the Dweller. But it is on the path of discipleship when the disciple becomes "occultly aware of himself" and he consciously begins to become mentally polarized. At that point, a condition in consciousness for the disciple is created whereby illusion, glamour and maya are seen as encompassing his entire life. For the disciple, he must recognize and master these energies and approach it with discrimination and discipline in meditation.

The disciple experiences the Dweller during the following stages of awareness:

- Stage of cleavage. At this stage, a growing cleavage in consciousness develops in the disciple and he is motivated in two directions: either towards personal ambition and personal desires or, moving himself towards the higher realms of the Soul and the Portal of Initiation.

- The stage where the Dweller is considerably tamed and the disciple consciously works in cooperation with the Soul. Here it is still recognized as a barrier to spiritual progress, and is influenced by the Soul rather than the lower nature.

The disciple's personality in combination with the sensed subtle energies of the Soul must create a stable consciousness by learning to *"hold the mind steady in the light"* thereby controlling his lower nature. This will allow the Divine Will to begin to control the disciple's nature resulting in the dissipation of the Dweller's power.

With a considerable control of the Dweller in consciousness, the "Angel of the Presence" or Solar Angel comes into awareness. The Angel represents future spiritual possibility as a revealer of divinity so that illumination can come forth into the disciple's consciousness.

The Dweller acting as a counterbalance presents itself as all the accumulated limitations, selfish habits, desires and tendencies. Using discrimination and correct orientation, the disciple becomes the initiate and confronts and reconciles any tensions and opposing forces in his mind – as he knows there is no separation in consciousness.

With the two forces in consciousness, he demands more light, more power, more understanding and desire for liberation for taking his next step forward. This results in the lower and higher minds becoming blended and fused as one. The Angel disappears, so that nothing is left but conscious knowledge and realization. The pure spirit of the Monad now exerts full control and at-one-ment takes place.

Note, it is not the Angel nor the Dweller, but the spiritual man himself who has to employ the higher will, and must solve this mystery of fusion alone. When he makes this demand with firmness in consciousness, and has no fear, the Angel will come forth. The Tibetan offers a clue that the disciple himself must have the capacity to discriminate the *"essential light and divinity hidden deep within the recesses of the dweller, and to bring such light forward in offering to the Solar Angel"*...thus creating a merging.

# Setting Up a Spiritual Practice

When you are serious about your personal transformation, you will create your own spiritual practice. Establishing a practice will greatly enhance spiritual transformation.

There are thousands of types of practices one can adopt. A paramount question for the spiritual seeker to ask is: *"What is the benefit of a spiritual practice?"* With the Soul as the guide, it helps you through every possible trial and growth, and every expansion of consciousness, up to final liberation.

This chapter covers the 3 main pillars of a spiritual practice: *meditation, spiritual study, and selfless service*. This description is described in many spiritual texts, e.g. the "Yoga Sutras of Patanjali" dating back over 2000 years. Employing this ancient formula, you will unite the body, the mind, the emotional-astral, and Soul into a working unity.

At some point, you will realize there is no separation between what you know, how you perceive yourself, and the actions you take. An effective spiritual practice will also reveal 'Who you are,' and 'Who you are not.' This is a nod to the spiritual axiom: "Know Thyself" at all levels of awareness.

Combining these 3 aspects allows you to come to recognize that your thoughts, feelings and expression of will are expressions of energy and force. With this knowledge it brings to the realization and expanded awareness about the nature of your existence and how you interact with the world.

Implementing the 3 pillars, it becomes a process of integration of the personality with the Soul, and later with Pure Spirit, the Monad. By fully embracing and incorporating all aspects of a spiritual practice, you are developing a "livingness" of Soul consciousness in your life.

**Setting Goals and Nurturing the Practice**

Here are some initial goals to work towards:

- A spiritual practice is a discipline, and it must be nurtured. Using meditation, you will learn to integrate the mental, emotional / astral, and physical-etheric bodies into one functioning unit as an act of will with the Soul.

- Learn to acquire an intelligent or "mental" understanding of how the heart (through love) and mind (through right thinking) work together expressing a more harmless, caring and loving behavior. Known esoterically as "love-wisdom", this is most readily facilitated by an integration of Soul values, e.g. cooperation goodwill and harmlessness.

- Having a spiritual practice will help to balance and stabilize the emotional and thought life in subtle ways with the Soul, just by its contact. By learning about energy vibrations and patterns, any limitations in consciousness are transformed.

- As you are purifying anything that blocks your true nature, you will also be cultivating a discerning mind. Keeping a spiritual journal is an effective tool for observing and studying the effects of harmlessness, anger and fear in your consciousness. Train yourself to become the Observer in both spiritual study and meditation.

- While contacting your Soul and integrating its values, your capacity for greater service expands. You will come to realize your purpose in the world is not just to evolve your own personal processes, but to help humanity grow into a more prosperous and creative civilization.

# Meditation

## The Science of Union

Meditation removes all layers of ego. Deep within our mind, we find our true nature the Soul.

The science of union is an ancient spiritual concept about blending the lower matter of the mental, emotional-astral and physical bodies of the personality with higher vibrational matter of the Soul or the Divine. The word yoga in Sanskrit means "union". Yoga here has two meanings: union with the Divine and as a means towards that union.

The object of this practice is to describe rules for achieving unification with the Divine through prescribed discipline and techniques. These will allow you to reach the highest spiritual development. In this work, you are consciously bringing together parallel forces in an effort to train the consciousness to act as One. This inevitably will result in purification of the mind and the body through a process of transference, transmutation and transformation.

In esotericism, these processes occur through the practice of Raja Yoga. This is a practice of self-discipline, discernment, discrimination, and purification. Transference involves the thinker consciously changing the flow of a lower vibration of thought and feeling to a higher vibratory quality of the Soul. This activity causes a "transmutation and transformation" in thought which results in an alignment of the concrete mind, the establishment of rational thinking, and a balance of emotional-astral with the physical-etheric nature.

With this practice, you the aspirant will be able to align the mind towards becoming rightly oriented with the higher vibrational energy patterns of the Soul.

## The Practice of "Esoteric" Meditation

For anybody wanting to consciously tread the spiritual path, learning to meditate is a must. Meditation is the best way to integrate your mental-emotional and physical-etheric form (i.e. the 3-Fold personality) into a sensed "oneness" with the Soul.

Meditation describes a process of how to experience the mind in its true or *natural state*. In this philosophy about meditation, you are not trying to create a peaceful state necessarily, although this is a by-product. You are creating a "direct experience" of who you truly are in your natural state, which is the Soul's consciousness.

The practice of esoteric meditation directly connects you with the Soul. The term "esoteric meditation" is used to infer that you will be encountering various thoughts, emotional energies, and other forces. As an esotericist you are ever *mindful* of completely subduing any emotional reactivity. You will want to negate anger, separatism and a "me only" mindset in order to create a stable consciousness free from these distractions.

A daily meditation practice will eventually help to establish a continuity of consciousness with the Soul. This will not happen immediately, but gradually over long periods of time.

A well-trained mind free of fears, anger, and selfishness will be able to better perform selfless service. With a stabilized consciousness, you will learn to live life consciously, spreading your light, love, and wisdom without any consideration of how much you give. In this way you have become a living example of the teachings.

Through these methods, you will learn how to transform the mind so that it can be a useful tool for expressing the Soul's purpose, which is service.

Transforming the Inner Realm

When going into meditation and entering the realm of your inner mind, it is wise to have an awareness about your tendencies in relation to the higher self, and its virtues.

In this space you are learning:

- About who you are, who you are not, and about the forces that make you up.
- Using mental techniques (see Appendix A), you are transforming the mind. When you begin to change the reality within, you will note changes in the outer environment of your thoughts and feelings, and how they play out with the people you encounter. It is not enough to just *feel good* after meditation. You will want to learn to remove all things that keep you from being peaceful, contented, and creative.
- The inner world of your mind is the place where ideas begin and conflicts are resolved. Meditation prepares your mind for practicing discrimination on different levels of the mental plane and for the purpose of expanding your consciousness. When you are not distracted with dark, separative, and selfish thoughts, which most people have, you can expand your creative inner world and find it to be a remarkably vital and transformative space.

**Purpose and Goals in Meditation**

Your purpose in meditating is to establish and maintain a direct connection with the Soul. To do this it is important to identify realistic goals and conduct an honest assessment of yourself by asking the following questions:

- *Why are you meditating? What are your motives, attitude, goals and purpose as you enter meditation?*

Answering this helps you to establish a "mental approach" and learn to practice conscious awareness in all your mental activities.

- *What keeps you from realizing the oneness with your Soul?* If you find a limitation, such as a fear, anger, etc., then what are you doing about transforming the energy?

Goals to Achieve:

- An initial goal of meditation is to create an alignment of the 3-Fold personality and see yourself as one with the Soul. Learn to integrate these three major parts of the personality and see it as a complete functioning unit, or an *integrated personality*. This will happen in stages.
- Identify with the concept that the Soul's energy is a "tension" and light (i.e. intelligence) in consciousness. Learn to stabilize you mind and hold this tension "steady in the light" of the Soul.
- A more advanced goal to learn would be to directly experience the Soul's consciousness as a state of beingness and pure awareness without thought. This will entail developing an inner capacity for inner seeing, listening and connecting with the Plane of the Intuition. As you progress on the Path, you will learn that observation and listening are very similar, e.g. meditate in silence and "listen"....for impressions from the Higher Self.

## Prerequisites for Meditation

Many meditators fail to make real progress because they do not pay attention to the prerequisites for developing good concentration, which is critical before meditation can begin. You will discover that meditation begins *once concentration has been established*. You will understand that actual meditation is a state of consciousness wherein you retrieve information directly from the Soul, or Buddhic Plane after reaching a meditative state. The information can typically be in the form of impressions, or impulses due to a direct communication with the Soul.

The following is designed to be very practical and is an ancient method for providing an essential teaching on meditative concentration. To establish a good foundation for a meditation practice, the meditator will want to follow the guidelines listed below:

- Calm space – noise free and peaceful surroundings, e.g. turn off your phone.

- Have few wants or desires – as desires keep the mind agitated and unhappy.

- Being content with your life's circumstances – the less we own and are responsible for, the less trouble in the mind.

- Life of pure ethics – for example right living and harmlessness. Needless to say, harmful activities in the heart or mind will greatly disturb the mind, such as lying, stealing, or sexual misconduct. These actions create karma and negatively impact the mind.

- Stop the flow of intellectual thought – this has to do with fantasy-daydreaming, intellectualizing the teachings, and thinking using the finite ego. The nuance here is that the meditator is using his imagination for fantasy purposes, and is intending on focusing on making Soul contact. If for instance you the meditator are using visualization, this activity can help bring the mind in alignment with the Soul. Another nuance is if you are thinking in *intellectual or worldly ways, this will* keep your consciousness associated with "all things" of the lower mental plane. Part of the goal is first to experience the higher abstract mind and make contact with the Soul, then connect higher still with the realms of the Buddhic Plane, and beyond.

- Posture: It's best to place the body in a upright position where the body is relaxed, but cannot fall asleep. The vertical uprightness of the body allows for the etheric energies between and around the chakras to flow properly. One of the goals in meditation is to establish the intuition and to practice conscious awareness. Right posture will directly aid in this process.

- Self-Observation: This is an activity of directed attention where we observe the thoughts and feelings that impede our concentration practice.

Object of concentration: A well-established concentration practice is the ground from which the flower of meditation can expand. This is done by directing the attention towards an object in meditation. Concentration becomes a method for attaining knowledge and acts as an instrument of illumination.

It's important to point out that concentration is not meditation. Concentration is used to initially focus and discipline the mind and hold your initial focus and to develop comprehension.

Focus your attention towards an object to aid in focusing the mind....to prepare for meditation.

- A *sacred image* (e.g., a candle, or a picture or image of Evolved Being)
- Focus on the breath (e.g., pranayama or rhythmic breathing)....this can create a calming sensation in the mind and etheric and physical form.
- Sounding To deepen your meditation, you can use a seed thought e.g. affirmation, mantra or chant. For example:
  o "I and my Soul are One", "I am love, truth, and beauty".
  o This exercise can be useful to eliminate hang-ups, angers and fears. You will have to experiment to find out what's right for you.
  o Meditation begins after the tension of concentration is released.
  At that moment there is no thought of feeling but a "SPACE" in awareness between them.

That space is a state of awareness and beingness. It is a significant goal to achieve.

o After reaching a meditative state, you can retrieve impulses coming from the Soul. These can be impressions, ideas, insights, wisdom, or guidance.

**Comprehension**

We have examined hinderances and obstacles. As you are moving on the path, you want to have a deeper understanding about your integration with the Soul. Observation here does not necessarily have to be in or during meditation. It can also be in quiet reflection during spiritual study or attentiveness in the waking mind.

You may ask yourself *what are you spiritually learning and comprehending?*

- It can be a teaching or more advanced study about learning how to control or re-pattern those thoughts that do not work for you.

  If you have an issue, look at yourself honestly and decide the best course of action. See also the section on "Spiritual Study" for more details.

- Mantrams and affirmations can help to focus thoughts for re-patterning or overcoming emotional hindrances. You many want to search out specific affirmations for focus on purifying the emotions and reactivity. Some suggested affirmations are included in Appendix A.

- Spiritual Study develops knowledge and Intuition. From this you gain experience and understanding or communication with the Soul that intuition is developing. You are sensing what and why you are doing something and determining the source of the material in question.

- Identification with thoughts and phenomena in your inner world, as part of yourself and not somebody else's. Be aware of this process and take responsibility.

- **Discrimination / Discernment** Learn to make wise conscious choices and become clear in thought and action. For example, learning about right and wrong. Ask: *"do I see this situation in stark terms or are there shades of gray?"*

Learn to *create a new intentionality* with your thoughts by making all of your life an activity of Soul purpose. Learn to trust the intuition.

In advanced stages of meditation, this awareness becomes more regular and inevitably will become a "Continuity of Consciousness".

- After a measure of purification, you can begin to experience a pure Awareness and a direct experience of your higher Self in its natural state – free of the distractions of the lower distracting energies.

- You begin to see that you have a choice and that you do not have to be controlled or disrupted from every thought of feeling. Thus, you can learn to hold your consciousness peacefully. The meditation process is also a means to slow down and observe how the mind works.

# Spiritual Study

*"Say not, I have found the path of the Soul. Say rather, I have found the soul walking upon my path. For the Soul walks upon all paths. The soul walks not upon a line, neither does it grow like a reed. The soul unfolds itself, like a lotus of countless petals."*

Kahlil Gibran

### Studying Spiritual Texts

*You may ask "Why should I study "X" text or "Which spiritual texts or readings should I study"?....or How should I study a spiritual text?*

We understand that the esotericist is self-taught and takes a mental attitude towards study. In approaching the subject of spiritual study, you start with the idea that you are wanting to stimulate the brain and mind so it can become open to impressions. Keep in mind that spiritual study can be complemented with the practice of meditation.

With this work your goal will be to develop pure reason, comprehension and discernment. Studying spiritual texts in this way stimulates deeper levels of the mind. This is a type of intuitive, synthetic understanding and is stimulated by the energies of the Soul and the buddhic plane, which you are developing in meditation.

Prior to study, it is recommended to align with the Soul and pose questions for setting the conditions for optimal comprehension. As a spiritual seeker, this is a form of *enquiring the way* towards "Self" understanding.

In this book, some of the following topics are discussed:

- Evolution of Consciousness and the Path of Liberation.
- Human Constitution. This is made up of the mental, emotional and physical - etheric bodies.
- Learning how to function as the Observer in meditation.
- The Science of Meditation.
- Purification of thought...understanding the dynamics dark side of thought; concept of harmfulness vs. harmlessness.

From any one of these subjects you can choose to delve deeper into understanding how these effect for example, the bodies of the personality (i.e. the mental, emotional and physical) and function within your consciousness. Authors of spiritual texts can include: Helena P. Blavatsky – "The Secret Doctrine", the Blue Books by Alice A. Bailey, books of Torkom Saraydarian, Sri Aurobindo, Thomas Merton, Geoffery Barborka, and many Buddhist, and Hindu texts. This can also include a study of the Yoga Sutras. Other related texts disseminating spiritual practice knowledge would be by Rosicrucian's, Manly P. Hall and Agni Yoga. Any of these can provide considerable information on these subjects on how to expand your consciousness.

Concurrent to spiritual study, you are seeking to bring the mental, emotional and physical bodies into an alignment with your Soul.

- Thus, studying spiritual texts stimulates the intuition, which you are developing in meditation.
- Esoteric studies will focus on developing, and unfolding the Soul aspect and revealing new opportunities for service.
- In your quiet reflective time, learn to use your thoughts and feelings wisely by asking questions about your purpose and discovering meaning and deeper subjective parts of yourself – as a Soul.
- If you look for teachers and teachings outside yourself, you will come to understand that meditation and spiritual study

will aid you in realizing that these show you 'truths' about your own inner realizations and knowingness.

- Think of this as providing you with a well-rounded *spiritual education*.

## Suggested Topics for Spiritual Study

The following suggested "stand alone" topics are presented for spiritual study. Incorporating any of these ideas can enhance your regular practice. From you own previous spiritual path and studies, you may already have been exposed to spiritual texts or information that have personal meaning to you. Whatever these are, they too can be used to stimulate and cause expansion of your awareness.

## Mindfulness

Mindfulness is a mental state that the individual achieves by focusing his awareness in the present moment. During this time, he may be aware of his feelings, thoughts, physical sensations, or even his psychic senses. This can possibly become an important practice when in an environment where safety or discernment is important or before making an important decision.

Practicing mindfulness can involve:

- Relaxation – of thoughts and body; Identify those things in the environment that cause anxiety, restlessness, and pain. Become conscious of patterns in thought and action, and make changes as it feels right.

- Learning to be aware of physical surroundings for understanding, safety, sounds, light (or lack of). This can be a developed awareness of anything that affects and effects the consciousness;

- Breathing – focusing on the breath can help to bring his awareness present;

- Regulation of emotions – for calming feelings of the astral nature;

- Practiced Awareness – Awareness of what is your consciousness "tending towards", such as a new life direction?

Four Goals for Mindfulness

1. ...of the physical body. Awareness of problems areas and need to attend to them. Awareness of keeping the body fit as a useful vehicle for the Soul in service.
2. ...of feelings. Practice an awareness of emotions when with others, or when watching the news note where your awareness are. Ask, *are you being reactive with your emotions or are you responding?*
3. ...of mental states and patterns of thought. Awareness of whether you are functioning in the concrete or abstract mind, and are open to impression.
4. ...of mental qualities. This develops the mental qualities of discernment, observation, and dispassion when viewing circumstances or a situation.

## Practice of Harmlessness

On the spiritual path there are many higher Soul qualities to cultivate and embrace. Among one of the most important is "harmlessness". Harmlessness is a mindset that should be cultivated often. It is important to bring forth and hold this awareness in consciousness for all encounters with people and situations in his environment.

There is a saying:

*"You cannot approach the Master until you have lost the power to wound or do harm"*....this is in thought and action, and necessitates a re-alignment of the personality towards harmlessness.

The energies of practiced harmlessness and goodness act as a primary driving energies. These influence you by expressing cooperation, love, goodwill, understanding, altruism, compassion, generosity, sharing, joy and kindness in all actions – both physical and verbal. It is an attitude of one who lives consciously as a Soul, whose natural inclination is love, and whose method is inclusiveness, not separation.

In the world today, harmlessness is demonstrated by an individual with right motive, practiced goodwill, and the ability to not engage in impulsive action or speech. The use of harmlessness in action and speech goes a long way towards fostering openness to communication, trust and understanding. On the other hand, a person with a 'harmful' attitude usually has a selfish ego-centric nature and causes separation.

Harmlessness is a mindset and practice that is important to bring forth for all encounters with people and situations in your life. Why? When connecting with the Soul you will quickly find that its nature is of love and goodwill. The practice of harmlessness is a bridge to the higher planes and spiritual growth.

It is recommended and instructive to study yourself and see how the different effects of *harmfulness* and *harmlessness* have on others. This can be done during meditation, or an evening review by analyzing the following:

Harmlessness in Thought:
- This is making the effort to eliminate harmful states of thinking. This enables thoughts about yourself and others that are positive and constructive.
  - The esotericist is one who is aware of the effects of forces and energies in the environment and on people. He knows and understands the appropriate use of the mind. It is for creating thoughts to carry out the Soul's purpose, and not for the selfish needs of the separated personality.

This Soul-driven mindset allows him to know that <u>he</u> <u>should never force himself</u> on others while engaging in any activity.

o The old esoteric axiom says *energy follows thought.* This means whatever he focuses his attention on, or in whatever direction his mind goes, so will be the direction of his thinking.

He is thinking *"I want to get 'X' for my own self,"* then these thoughts in combination with will and desire, will drive him to carry out his task, regardless of whether he creates karma for himself. In short, he brings life and vitality to his thoughts.

o Harmlessness brings caution in judgment, reticence of speech, ability to refrain from impulsive action, and a demonstration of a non-critical spirit.

o In esotericism, the aspirant is motivated by the energy and thought of goodness. This can be understood as both energy and force to help enable positive change and benefit for an individual, society, or civilization. When practiced, it is goodwill or love in action.

o Harmlessness is an attitude of one who lives consciously as a Soul, whose natural inclination is love, and whose method is inclusiveness. This is love-wisdom and goodwill in action.

o Practiced harmlessness will orient the spiritual worker's values towards developing an attitude of helping others, and training himself not to act or say things of an impulsive or critical nature.

- Harmlessness in <u>Emotional</u> reaction
  o He studies his emotional effects on others so there is no mood, depression, nor emotional reaction that can harm his fellow man. Violent aspiration, misplaced, or misdirected energy may harm others, so he looks not

only at his wrong tendencies, but at the use of higher virtues to offset them.

- o A spiritual journal can also be a means for observing the effects of a harmful attitude, by studying the effects that anger and fear have on his consciousness.
- Harmlessness in Action
  - o In order to progress on the path, a good exercise would be to practice harmlessness until the aspirant has a firm rhythm established. In many instances, it requires self-knowledge and courage. Harmlessness is a mindset that should be cultivated often for all encounters with people and situations.
  - o If you are harmless in your actions, it would be of great benefit to remember how this looks and feels.

**Redemption / Reorientation of Personality Bodies**

While connecting with the Soul either through meditation or being the Observer, you are in fact redeeming and reorienting, i.e. upgrading your lower bodies. Probably most of the time, this happens in the background of your conscious mind.

When aligning your mind with the Soul, eventually the lower mind will become more Soul infused.

Here, the light of the Soul as an energy, is transforming your thoughts so you become a conscious creator in thought building.

Redemption in the esoteric context is an act of transformation of the etheric matter and energies of your 3-Fold nature, and replacing it with the higher / finer energies of buddhi from the Plane of the Intuition.

In practical terms, the energies of redemption and reorientation will over time transform any tendencies of harmfulness, selfishness, and irrational behavior. This will result in all lower emotional and mental plane reactivity becoming neutralized and raised up.

In this example, the emotional-astral substance is redeemed or upgraded, and is replaced with buddhi and pure reason from the Plane of Intuition. While in meditation, it is the Soul's light that does the job of redemption and transformation of the lower matter of the personality.

## Developing the Esoteric Sense

The term "esoteric sense" denotes a gradually developing spiritual power in the disciple, who is strongly at-one and aligned with the Soul.

The esoteric sense allows you to:

- Live and function subjectively on mental levels via the Soul and the lower planes of the personality. With this attitude, you are able to orient in both the inner and outer planes.

- Posses a constant inner contact in your waking state with the Soul. This marks a transcendence of personality issues and allows you to have complete control over your emotional life. As a result, you become a clearer instrument for enabling higher spiritual concepts and impressions to be registered in the mind.

- Actively demonstrate love and wisdom in all you do through goodwill and loving understanding.

- Mentally tune into the realms of thought and ideas. You can choose those mental concepts and ideals, which will be recognized in the world of everyday thinking, and living.

- Develop an attitude of mind where you will be able to orient yourself in that high place of inspiration and light. There you will communicate with and discover your fellow-workers as they will work together in implementing divine intentions.

The esoteric sense can be cultivated by holding the attitude of the Observer during meditation, spiritual study and in your waking state.

As time passes, you will realize that your meditations have caused you to grow spiritually and have enabled a strong spiritual orientation. This has resulted in you developing an attitude of the detached observer.

**Developing the World of Meaning**

Through study and analysis of spiritual teachings, the esotericist can bring inspiration to his life. When combined with meditation and spiritual living, spiritual study can help develop the world of meaning.

Daily stimulation of the mind and connecting with the Soul is necessary so it can become responsive to impressions and higher energies from the Soul.

Remember, an impression is an idea, feeling about something or someone, especially one formed without conscious thought. This can be a "first impression" of a person or place that is sensed on the inner planes.

- The impression by its very form is of a subjective nature, and is closely aligned with the intuition. Impressions often come in the form of symbols, or an image, and register in the concrete mind as an idea, or thought.

- As an esotericist, observe that people covey thoughts through voice, body language, or even in print, such as online blogs, magazines and books. These are examples as subtle forms of telepathy that are conveying thought energy. Learn to be a conscious aspirant as a sensitive receiver of impulses from outside sources.

   These other "voices" are thought energies to become sensitive to while responding.

This could also be called spiritual reading where you are looking at outer events and life's circumstances, and deriving meaning.

- The highest response is the intuition, as this infers you are making a connection with the higher mind, such as connecting with the Buddhic Plane. There pure reason, "knowingness", and truth are registered.

By studying, reading, and contemplating spiritually related material, the aspirant's capacity to rationalize and reason *wisely* increases. He will open yourself to other ways of thinking, and varying points of view. He will open himself in developing the capacity to filter, choose, and make his own conclusions, using discrimination and discernment.

## Listening

Listening is not just the hearing sounds with your ears, but the establishment of a constructive state of mind. For the esotericist this involves stilling the lesser concrete mind of thought and feeling to becoming aware of impressions and impulses from the Soul or Master.

As he practices discernment, he is listening for guidance and impression and thus becomes receptive to what he hears.

It is the cultivation of an awareness of what is occurring in consciousness. This process can be aided through the practice of discernment and discrimination.

Through the power of listening, the disciple learns:

- The nature of the teachings he is studying.

- Benefits gained by applying the teaching.

- Drawbacks by not applying the teaching.

- How obstacles can be removed by the teaching.

The means by which applying the teaching produces the desired end result.

## Practice "Livingness"

When the spiritual seeker is consciously holding Soul consciousness while engaged in a service related activity, that connection has a "living" quality to it. What is the nature of *livingness?*

In essence, "livingness" is that Soul energy, of light and love moving through your consciousness freely in all activities.

Livingness is also a *prompting* energy to practice harmlessness, integrity and compassion with individuals and groups. But it is more than just an awareness. It is a vitalizing energy and consciousness of the Soul that is held. It can be thought of also as a presence always in the background. With this, you make the effort to identify with that Soul energy, then you are guided and can set your intentionality from that place. This energy gives you purpose, intention and direction when it is present.

Living for the purpose of the Soul, means that "living energy of the Soul" becomes transformed into purpose and will shine on others.

## Spiritual Values to Live By

After the spiritual seeker progresses a certain distance on the path, the channels for impression and intuition from the Soul can open up. The higher energies of the Soul are felt and these in turn have a direct effect on the mental, emotional and physical bodies.

These higher energies can include:
- Love of Truth – essential for an inclusive and progressive society;
- Spirit of Cooperation - through practiced and active goodwill and right human relations;
- Sense of Justice – recognition of rights and needs for all;

- Sense of Personal Responsibility – Of self, for the group, Community and National affairs;
- Harmlessness in all thought and action.

As mentioned earlier, meditation directly connects the spiritual seeker with the Soul through the Abstract mind with the purpose of holding these values for greater service.

## Use of the Will

An initial discussion on the will is about whether you are driven by Divine will or your own Freewill.

Divine Will

The higher Will coming from the Soul and higher sources and represents the "Will-to-Good" expressed as divine ideation. It is stepped down by Hierarchy or Masters to humanity, and manifests as 3 Aspects: Will / Purpose, Love-Wisdom, and Active Intelligence.

As the spiritual seeker evolves and his personality is becoming integrated with the Soul, he learns how the Divine Will works in his consciousness through observing the power of his own will.
By "Knowing Yourself" and all that entails in consciousness, you are training yourself to carry out the higher will in service.

Freewill

- The concept of human freewill is closely linked to the concepts of moral responsibility, praise, guilt, sin, and other judgements which apply only to actions that are freely chosen. It is also connected with the concepts of advice, persuasion, deliberation, and prohibition.
- You may be consciously aware of different forces in your environment, some of which may be beyond your control. In the world, freewill has been focused around expressing authoritative control over others through dogma, ideology.
- In the world, freewill has been focused around expressing authoritative control over others through dogma and

authoritarian ideology. We see this in government, the work place, and generally in the public sphere. There are obvious positives and negatives here.

- Obviously when wills are opposing each other, there are clashes, leading to crisis. Solutions and change can depend on the strength of a single person or a group united in a common cause.

We see this all the time by people who have expressed their will and influence local, national, and international affairs.

- When man becomes spiritually awake, he can use his skill or knowledge to put himself in a position where he can influence as a force for good, simply by an act of will with his mind and action.
- The "conscious" spiritual seeker carries out his activities guided by the Will-to-Good with a definite goal to be achieved. In this way, he or she acts as a Soul-conscious entity that requires him to think in terms of expressing and manifesting divine intent.

Other Forms of Will

- Within the Cosmic Physical Plane, the Monad or pure Spirit expresses a much higher aspect of will for man through the planes of Atma, Buddhic and Manasic. It is the Soul through multiple incarnations, that trains the personality through impression.
- In an esoteric context, people can meet and use their wills for meditation and provide influence on the inner planes, such as through meditation for healing and prayer work. This type of expression constitutes an expression of spiritual force.

## Wisdom from the Yoga Sutras

In the section "Purification and Obstacles to Overcome", we discussed that a hindrance can be any action, thought, or emotion that prevents, delays or interferes with the aspirant from directly connecting with the pure nature of Soul. It can also be an energy, such as a glamour or illusion (i.e. a set of thoughts) that keeps him from knowing a higher truth, or practicing a virtue.

From the Yoga Sutras by Patanjali, obstacles and hinderances are overcome by practicing what are called "yamas" and their complement the "niyamas".

These represent a series of ethical rules, commandments or goals for "right living". Yamas and niyamas represent commitments that affect one's relations with the self and others. These are considered to be the first two practices for working with the inner self in moving towards spiritual union.

Sanskrit: <u>Yamas</u> are the ethical principles that deal with one's behavior and how one interacts with the outer world. These guide the student to follow for proper conduct, such as practicing harmlessness and becoming non-reactive.

The 5 commandments or yamas are:

1. <u>Harmlessness</u>: Principle of nonviolence, non-harming of other living beings;
2. <u>Truth</u>: Concerns the use of speech....*"before the voice can speak in the presence of the Master, it must have lost the power to wound."*. truthfulness, non-falsehood;
3. <u>Abstention from theft</u>: non-stealing (physical and in thought);
4. <u>Abstention from incontinence</u>: this is desirelessness of any out-going (verbal and physical) tendencies and impulses of physical expression in relation to the sexes. Other tendencies of incontinence include pleasure seeking to satisfy the desire nature;

5. <u>Abstention from Avarice:</u> this relates to the sin of covetousness or the concept of theft on the mental plane. It concerns the use of mental energy that you do not take anything, i.e. physical or intangible that is not rightly yours.

Sanskrit: Niyamas refer to "reining in", "restraint" or "control" of oneself as the spiritual seeker practices ethical rules for "right living". The 5 Rules or niyamas are:

1. <u>Self-Purification</u> means "purification; cleanliness of the body."

   Relates to the 3 sheaths of the lower 3-Fold bodies and interpreted in a dual sense. Each sheath should be kept clean and free of impurities. This then becomes a study of what the individual attracts to himself.

2. <u>Contentment</u> means "acceptance, satisfaction, delight, happiness, joy in one's life;

   Understanding that one's life conditions and environment are regarded as correct and serve the aspirant best for working out his problems and achieving his goals in life. It is a recognition of one's present assets and opportunities that form a background for future progress.

3. <u>Fiery Aspiration</u> means "to heal" and infers an inner austerity and passion towards one's practice;

   This refers to the fiery mental effort and steady persistence to fulfilling the ideal and understood in discipleship. This leads to a constant discipling of the physical form, steadiness of the emotional and an attitude in the mind enduring faithfulness.

   This leads to transformations and purifies the individual allowing his conscious awareness to control unconscious impulses and poor behavior.

4. Self-Study or Spiritual Reading connotes a study and observation of the subjective realities of the self.

   Deep introspection and discernment are used to determine the cause behind all desires, aspirations and feelings. This is the ability to see divine lessons through contemplation of life's lessons and through meditation on the "truths" demonstrated by great Teachers.

5. Self-Surrender constitutes a heartfelt attitude and dedication of the lower 3-Fold self, brought into obedience towards the Soul or Master.

**Practical Use of a Spiritual Journal and Evening Review**

This book emphasizes the notion that the esotericist is self-taught, which is an ancient concept and is profoundly true. You learn to be constantly focused on understanding whatever comes up in your consciousness. This implies you will study spiritual texts, or use meditation as a means for understanding a situation or a relationship to a particular energy.

A spiritual journal and evening review can enhance this process if it is frequently maintained. It allows you to mull over ideas and concepts experienced during the day. Over time, the journal becomes a record of previous experiences, observations, impressions, dreams, etc., which can be referenced.

Your journal will be used to note all changes in consciousness that occur around spiritual study, and meditation, including encounters with other people.

This style of note taking is important, as it helps you understand what is happening in your own mind, allowing you to identify patterns of thought, and recognize the world of the Soul emerging in your consciousness.

This form of observation can be particularly useful when practiced over a period of time. This become a record, so you can look back on particular happenings, and study recurring patterns. Seeing patterns that may emerge in consciousness allows you to interpret what was written before, and use the intuition to come up with a strategy for growth and transformation of a thought or feeling. Besides the types of journal entries noted above, previous entries can be useful when you want to integrate a new concept or idea in your life, or even act on an impression.

Some suggested entries can be:

- Impressions, ideas – *Can you trace their origin? Is the impression or idea clear?*

- Significant events or situations where there is an astral-emotional component. Study how and why you participate.

- Significant dreams - note your immediate impressions of the dream and its meaning. *Are there any noteworthy symbols?* Symbols can also be a means of Soul contact.

Although this presents the view that many dreams come from the subconscious mind, it can mean that there are lots of potential unresolved emotional-astral issues. Nevertheless, this can be a useful exercise if you are willing to deal with and purify that part of your mind.

Suggested Strategies

For example.....an individual knows he has a fear of public speaking. As he noted in his journal before, the fear comes from an earlier time in his life. This fear holds him back from growing in his service work. Now what's new is that he just got an interesting idea or impression telling him to use public speaking as a means for getting past the fear. In this example he knows he must challenge himself to transform the energy of fear. So, with a measure of courage, he gives public talks, and over time the fear dissipates. By getting past the fear, his Soul's radiance can now flow better through him, and his service work is enhanced.

If the aspirant has a good understanding of the problem, he can learn to use his intuition to develop further insight. If there are additional hindrances and even potential crises, then he can learn to move through them and develop a strategy for preventing it from happening *that way* again.

One of goals the aspirant should learn is to use energy and force *efficiently* and *wisely*. In the example above, he stood back and studied the power and effect of the fear, and how he ultimately transformed the limiting energy. As he takes notes in his journal, it helps him to develop his skills in studying the effects of energy and force. He may study it and ask:

> *With what I know of the situation, how  can I make this work in a better way?* or

> *What worked, or did not work well, and why?*

The process described above is to study a problem and develop a strategy using a 'mental' approach. This allows him to act as the observer to work with both the lower and abstract minds.

Later, through meditation, he will ultimately develop 'pure reason.' This is a type of intuitive, synthetic understanding stimulated by the energies of the Buddhic Plane.

He needs to train himself to conduct his life *as if* in a meditation, practicing mindfulness and sensitivity to the Soul's impressions.

This gives him the opportunity to keep pace with the Soul's intent and motive, which is to grow, learn, and be joyful in the process. When he has blended buddhi with the lower 3-fold nature, e.g., intuition with the mental and emotional, you will be able to a clearer vision of the whole, and your relationship of every part to that whole. This will enable him to think and act with wisdom.

Down the road, this understanding will help to ultimately establish a *'continuity in consciousness'* or allow the Soul's light to freely flow through his consciousness.

## Understanding the Various States of Mind

Over the long course of the aspirant's spiritual journey he will experience various states of mind. He will be particularly aware of these states when purifying and expanding his consciousness.

For the esotericist, it is an important exercise to study and understand how these interact with his consciousness. He will immediately see that the concept of duality plays a major part of something that he must eventually learn to transcend.

Initially, the aspirant must learn to align and hold his awareness in the spiritual center of the Soul's consciousness as a *felt spiritual tension*. These energies can help develop the mind. In advanced stages of spiritual development and meditation, the aspirant will reach a point in his consciousness where nothing can pull him from his center. He will know that the center of his consciousness is one with the Soul where there is no conflict and serenity abides.

Serenity and pure beingness are states of mind characteristic of the buddhic plane. Here, the knower allows no disturbances, emotions or thoughts of separation from his lower self. He realizes that all disturbances come from a mindset of separation of the personality, or the *not-self*.

At that higher point in consciousness, any illusions are experienced, transmuted, or transformed into love, and aspiration. His identification has moved from the selfish solar plexus 'I' consciousness to being immersed in the Soul's consciousness.

Besides love, there are other terms used in many spiritual conversations, which have their parallels, but sometimes get confused with love. They are: Happiness, Peace, Joy, Serenity, and Bliss.

Happiness

The feeling of happiness has its base in the emotions of the astral body, and is usually understood to be a personality reaction. Happiness is dualistic in nature and is almost always in contrast to *unhappiness.* It occurs when the personality has created the conditions, which make its lesser nature feel satisfied and content.

It manifests as a sense of physical and emotional well being, through contentment with one's surroundings, with other people, and with significant life opportunities.

Happiness is felt through the lower mental, emotional, and physical bodies, and is the goal of the separated personality. If the individual has developed an inner spiritual connection with the Soul, the feeling of happiness is conveyed through a feeling of unity and contentment.

Many people have discovered through the *new science of happiness* that performing acts of kindness, sometimes randomly, results in creating more happiness.

Peace

As stated with happiness, peace is also understood to having a dualistic understanding where the personality seeks freedom from suffering, inner conflict, or turmoil.

Initially, we understand peace to emanate from the emotional-astral levels or lower mental planes, thus it has a strictly worldly context.

From several online dictionaries, we find the word *peace* to have at least two basic meanings:

- Freedom from disturbance, and
- Freedom from or the cessation of war or violence

As the aspirant's personality begins to align and connect with the Soul, he learns to quell his lesser nature, which is often fraught with conflict and turmoil. When this happens, the separated personality naturally seeks respite as a goal.

It should be noted that while peace is a goal for the separated personality be it personal or worldly, it will still attract its opposite, conflict.

Later, after his own personal evolution progresses, he will make connections with the higher buddhic energy, and come to experience *serenity* was a place in consciousness where there is *no duality or conflict.*

Serenity

There is no experience of serenity on the lower planes. It can only be *known* when the disciple connects with the buddhic plane and is able to focus or *"hold his mind steady in the light."* On the buddhic plane, there is a complete absence of duality, thoughts, conflict, desire, or turmoil. Thus serenity allows the aspirant to experience a state of pure *beingness* and "gnosis" or direct knowingness.

Joy

Joy infers an inner *knowingness* of the Soul and its consciousness. From the Ageless Wisdom Teachings, we find the term joy to mean:

- Joy is a quality of the Soul. It is felt and realized in the mind and heart when there is alignment between the personality and the Soul.

- Joy is a shared feeling when group consciousness, group oneness, and solidarity is felt and known.

- Joy is the feeling for the server, via the Soul, and is a result of pure "unselfish" service. If there is a regular practice of service to others, then the discipline of the service results in joy being the outcome.

## Bliss

Bliss, or the *state of bliss*, is associated with those individuals who are nearing liberation and are experiencing a form of ecstasy in consciousness.

It is generally considered to be the nature of Spirit or the Monad. For bliss to be experienced, the meditator must have at least achieved a oneness with the Soul and moved through the higher initiations.

# Service – the Impulse of Light

*Not everybody can be famous*

*But everybody can be great,*

*Because greatness is determined by service.*

~ Martin Luther King Jr.

The need to serve is a concept and impulse that has evolved in people and groups over time. This concept of helping people in crisis or need, or expressing service through intelligent loving or giving was for the most part, a very foreign concept to most people up until recent times.

Over the last 800 years or so, western civilization in part, evolved out of a new influx of light sensed by creative, courageous, and ambitious people from Europe and Asia. This new sensed light stimulated man's creativity, and opened up his mind through inquiry initiating revolutions in culture, science, the arts, and politics, which brought Humanity the Age of Exploration, the Renaissance and the Age of Enlightenment. Although it was a time of great openings and new inventions and ways of being, this was nevertheless an era of the individual.

Looking back over the centuries, we see that man's consciousness has evolved from the perspective in which only the needs of individual matter ....to the perspective in which we need to be concerned also for the larger community or group. In recent times, we have seen the emergence of a new way of approaching how the individual and the group function that is based upon the concept of service.

Through the awareness and implementation of the Ageless Wisdom teachings in its myriad forms, many enlightened servers are acting on the impulse of selfless service that involves helping the larger group and not just the individual.

Less than a century ago, the urge to serve was largely felt at the spiritual seeker's emotional level. In many instances feelings arose from a reaction to the problems of the day, and enabled him to have a tendency for laying blame for the deplorable conditions seen around the world caused by certain individuals, families, corporations, and nations.

## Service is Goodwill in Action

The Tibetan Master D.K. describes service as *the spontaneous effect of Soul contact*. It is an energy that demonstrates as the life of the Soul working within the personality's nature. It is the activity of intelligent loving and giving motivated through the expression of goodwill. The motivation to serve will not come from the spiritual seeker alone, as he must have Soul stimulation or inspiration. The term *service* denotes spiritual qualities and values, such as cooperation and goodwill emanating from the Soul, which are focused outwardly, but *known* by the spiritual seeker as an inner reality.

How effective you will be in your service work will be determined by the amount of integration and alignment of your lower three bodies with the Soul. If you are Soul integrated, then the Soul's light and love will pour more easily into your bodies. In this teaching and philosophy, it is understood that service *is not an activity*, nor something which people must do. Service is considered to be a *demonstration of the life of the Soul* as the service worker is allowing your personality to become a living channel and expression for the Soul on the physical plane.

In your meditations, Soul contact is made with an awareness that you are a *living principle of this harmony*. After a rhythm has been established, you begins to experience *"standing in spiritual being"*. The effect of this living energy will demonstrate as power (i.e., a force) and love (i.e. an energy) and *radiance* around others.

**Urge to Serve**

As the Soul is naturally group conscious, it impresses the spiritual seeker with the *urge to serve* and the spiritual seeker responds with the inner urge to cooperate, and as a result, implements the higher purposes of the group. In the outer world, we see that service is a powerful Soul expression for enabling *right* group relations.

As harmony becomes part of the natural expression of the personality, the server will naturally be practicing harmlessness. This energy breaks down blockages. For example, if the server is a facilitator of a group that has members with opposing viewpoints, his poise and expression of harmlessness will allow him not to take sides and be able to see a higher way for fostering mutual cooperation.

The outward expression of service is also a means par excellence for awakening people to their own spiritual consciousness, giving them a sense of responsibility for themselves and the greater group they are increasingly identifying with.

The server will offer help for others to know and understand what it means to *stand in spiritual being* as he himself has learned. He will aid individuals in expressing service in their chosen field as he or she desires to express it, and not dictating how and where service should be done.

**Serve from a Balanced Nature**

From a certain perspective, performing service is like putting on new clothes and requires a reorientation of the personality. Perhaps you are already engaged in service related activities? Your purpose here is to obtain a whole picture of what service can ideally look like as part of a spiritual practice.

Keep in mind that service itself is a result of an inner effect between the personality and the Soul. When this rapport is established, certain things occur in the personality.

A change in the personality awareness will occur when you have a tendency to turn away from the things of your personal self and re-focus on the larger issues of the needs of the group or community This results in a reorientation or decentralization of your personality. In a worldly context, this can also be letting go of addictions, whether minor or small, such as shopping, gambling, or food cravings. These are all distractions to the mind.

The true and conscious server will have achieved what could be called a 'spiritual balance' – this is part of a spiritual practice.

The seeker is aware of:

- _Where_ his consciousness is at any moment
- _What_ he is doing
- _Knowledge_ of the environment in which he is working, i.e. this is relating to the inner landscape of his mind
- Maintaining a connection with the Soul, knowing that this connection is a _spiritual tension._
- Spiritual tension originating from the Soul that has a _quality of radiance_ (and livingness), and can be used for outward expression of service and goodwill.

To be most effective in your work, study the energies and forces present in your consciousness and learn to bring balance within yourself. From his _balanced place_, you will radiate confidence from the Soul level, and help create an amicable outcome in whatever you do.

**Effects of Service**

When the Soul is beginning to transform the consciousness of the individual server, it is also beginning to affect the larger group of Humanity itself.

*How is it doing this?*

Since most people are not conscious of this inner connection with each other, we can nevertheless still experience others through telepathic and other psychic means. For these types of subjective connections, look at the concept of *"a national conversation"* on a political or social issue. For example, the "MeToo" Movement started when certain individuals were abusing other people, namely women. Or the "Black Lives Matter" Movement where police brutality towards black men or women has occurred for generations. The conversation continues with officials, the media and protests in the streets about what transpired. The very ideas discussed e*ffected our minds.*

We may have agreed or disagreed with outcomes, but the concepts were of a subjective nature and the effect is felt on the inner planes of the heart and the mind.

Another idea is *running after service,* for example, through will-nilly giving to philanthropic causes. Activities can interpreted by the personality, who seeks to impose his ideas of service upon others. Although the server is sensitive to impression, he, in the initial phases of Soul contact can misinterpret the truth. He must learn to identify with the unfolding Soul life and not just dwell on changing the outcomes only on the physical plane.

This concept is about the server being connected with his Soul, and learning to hold a 'spiritual mindset' in his life. In this way, he is responding spontaneously to service, as opposed to the mentality of: *"I think I'll engage in this activity because I think it is needed."* The type of service may indeed be needed, but the point here is to realize and know how much the personality is driving the decision process.

Knowing this can help to facilitate greater effectiveness in service work. Only by honestly looking at yourself, will you really be able to answer this.

## Upgrading or Training Your Bodies for Service

On the face of it, "Upgrading Your Bodies for Service" is a odd expression. When engaged in service you do not think about the conditioning of your mental, emotional and physical bodies. But there is a form of preparation and mindset of maintaining these bodies for service.

With regards to the physical body, you can keep your body fit by eating right, going to the gym, taking walks, riding a bike, or do whatever to maintain your physical body.....as it is your vehicle for physically performing service.

Emotional Preparation

The natural state of the Soul is calm, clear, and of pure awareness. For you the spiritual seeker, your intention should be to create a stable, quiet emotional vehicle for the Soul to flow through in all the activities you engage in, or with the people you meet.

Mental Preparation

For mental preparation, the mind must become stable, clear and in a *listening and observing mode.*

This entails:

- Being alert for impressions and subjective contact. This allows you to express higher values, such as cooperation and goodwill.

- Learning to make all of your life's experiences and activity that of the Soul's purpose by creating a new intentionality.

- Recognizing "Soul Awareness" as a connection and as a point of tension. Attempting to hold that tension or awareness in your conscious waking life, this is akin to developing a "continuity of consciousness".

○ This tension is developed through the practice of meditation, which allows for the livingness aspect of the Soul to freely move within the your consciousness.

When speaking of training, this is a reference to preparing the matter of the physical and etheric bodies for a connection with the Soul and performing service.

A body composed of "spiritually unprepared" lower and dense matter will prevent the aspirant from making contact with the higher vibration of the Soul. Keep in mind, that the higher vibration of the Soul would have virtually no impact on a non-evolved physical brain or etheric body.

To prepare and maintain the physical and etheric body to be an agile and useful tool for the Soul in service, it is recommended at a minimum that you have the following daily regimen in place:

- Pure and vital food: The individual must decide whether to eat pure foods, such as organic or a vegetarian diet – as feels appropriate;

- Cleanliness: Practice good hygiene to keep the body clean from disease;

- Sunshine: Take it in where and when it's healthy to do so, as it helps the body stay vitalized;

- Sleep: You must have enough sleep to enable you to carry out your spiritual work with the greatest facility.

  If the physical body is tired, or lacking in energy due to poor nutrition or not enough rest, then the body controls the situation and keeps you from making Soul contact and performing meaningful service.

Physical Exercise: Daily exercise or engaging in physical activity is important for maintaining a healthy body. Exercise will benefit to help overcome health conditions and diseases and help change one's mood.

- Besides diet and exercise helping in your overall well-being, it also helps you maintain a sound mental-emotional attitude for service.

- This overall mindset, provides you with an awareness that you are a fully unified Being expressing the Soul's intent moving through you.

## Inconvenience and the Path

This is a topic which many people have encountered, but rarely discussed. There are times in the individual's life when he must fulfill obligations and perform service. This means he must stop what he is doing and help somebody in need.

From a worldly point of view, a person will encounter situations where he must perform some activity, and say: *"I don't have the time, "this is not what I planned to be doing right now,....but I must."* So what are some of the <u>potential</u> energies happening in the person's consciousness?

Answer: *Anger, Resentment, Selfishness, and Impatience. These are the feelings of a personality, not Soul focused.*

A person who is Soul aligned will encounter similar situations of *inconvenience*, but have a different response. The reaction will not be anger or resentment, but love, gratitude, and perhaps even a sense of *flowing with,* or adapting to the situation. It is also knowing that service sometimes works by bringing the server to a particular place and allowing his Soul's radiance to be present. Ideally, you do not question the circumstance, but as a consciously aware and Soul-focused person, you understand that you are bound to bring forth the highest energies of love and the mindset *"I am a pure instrument of service."*

Another way of approaching the energy of "me only" mindset is to study your urges or motivations by noting them in a spiritual journal.

Ask yourself:

- *Do I tend towards thinking of myself in all circumstances, or do I embody compassion and kindness?*
- *What are my motivations?*
- *What are my first impulses when an opportunity to serve arises?*

To the server on the Path who understands these dynamics, he is ever vigilant and aware of the possibility for serving at a moment's notice.

Learn to ask yourself:

*"When so-and-so happens in my life, then what are the choices I am making?"*...and *Why?*

*"What am I bringing with me at any moment?"*

# Staying the Course

## Elimination of Discouragement

In 1999 a movie that came out called "Enlightenment Guaranteed". It is about two very different brothers in Berlin. One, who has been meditating for years wants to take a "spiritual vacation" to deepen his practice at a monastery in Japan. He has been meditating for years but doesn't realize that discipline is needed to make real progress. Upon his arrival in Japan, he has problems with the local culture, namely the language. The other brother, who has little or no spiritual training comes and rescues him, and both end up at a monastery. In short, it is the brother with little or no spiritual training who makes real spiritual progress with the teachers there. Why? Because he had no preconceived notions, was disciplined and was easily able to let go of any limitations in consciousness. For him, meditation came easy.

Perhaps, one point here might be to realize when connecting with your true spiritual essence, to let go of all limitations in order to make a deep connection with the Soul.

In considering the effort required to "tread the path" and make spiritual progress, one must have a realistic sense of the work ahead and be disciplined to carry it out. The most common factor in discouragement is due to the over development of the concrete mind. When you have too lofty or even unobtainable goals, then it puts a demand on the emotional nature and the physical body also suffers. In this case, it is wise to create a sense of balance by identifying realistic goals and allowing a mental equilibrium to be achieved.

During the path of integration, there are many opportunities for letting discouragement set in, such as wanting to progress on the path faster than is wise or realistic. It is best to *make haste slowly*" through developing quality in your nature (i.e. consciousness) with a sense of time.

As you are connected with the Soul in meditation, you know you are progressing one step at a time in time and evolution.

One cure for discouragement is to wisely use your mental body. This means maintaining a connection with the Soul as a tension, as much as you can in meditation and in your waking state. This will help you develop the capacity to reason logically, and to see the causes of problems that condition and effect your personality. If you sense you are pushing yourself too much in personal development, then establish a quietness within through contemplation, be patient, continue with your meditations, and let time become a great factor in attaining achievement.

During the transition period of balancing the emotional and mental natures, you still will have certain "habits of living". Discomfort can be felt with balancing feelings of love-hate, pain-pleasure, reactivity of emotions, and "want or "can't have" mindset. By Invoking the light of the Soul as a tension into your consciousness, this will purify your thoughts and feelings of any dark tendencies that nothing can disturb.

Training your mind to identify with Soul and not the personality, will in the long run alleviate the "suffering" quality of the personality. By decentralizing the personality, self-preoccupation will gradually lose its hold and fade. Learning about reactivity and responsiveness brings higher wisdom. As a new polarization and focus into the higher mind with the Soul takes place, you learn to become more evocative, thereby allowing the Soul's energies to flow through you. The Soul's nature is impressing you with ideas from Universal Mind and you are learning to be responsive for carrying out your higher impulses.

Discouragement can be countered by allowing a gradual unfoldment and tackling of each blockage and cleavage, so that you have a clear path to the Soul. You must learn to study and subordinate your own thoughts to the "pattern of things in the Heavens".

You must master each stage of integration and awareness to allow a gradual unfolding process. This will help cultivate your inner joy. The quality of the Soul is intelligence, love and will, whereas its nature is joy.

As an esotericist, learn to cultivate the following:

- Consecration of motive....Ask: how much is my personality involved vs. the Soul? As you understand your own motives and apparent needs, you will come to recognize and trust your higher inmost Self.
- Look for meaning beneath all appearances through action and relationships.
- Utter fearlessness....Learn to go forward with ideas, vision, and plans motivated by Soul intent.
- Frequently, "enquire the way" or ask *"is my thinking process coming from the higher mind and not the lower?"* The lower mind can help organize, but allow the higher mind to be the great source of vision and inspiration.
- Train yourself to observe whether you are emotionally reacting to people and situations or responding from mental levels.
- Learn to develop and cultivate the imagination, balanced wisely by the reasoning faculty.
- Learn to develop a mental capacity to wisely consider all factors for the considered course of action. This is being grounded in the mental and not the emotional plane. Accept only that which is compatible with the highest instinct and intuition, thus preventing rashness to enter.
- A willingness to experiment. "mentally know" there are different options. Wisely step back and weigh them and visualize a successful path forward.
- Learn to distinguish between essentials and non-essentials.

These tendencies, coupled with purity of life and regulation of thought will lead you to spiritual achievement.

## Strength and Courage

At times in your spiritual work "staying the course" and continuing may be difficult, and possibly even painful. This requires strength and courage. There are different kinds of courage, e.g. physical, emotional, moral and intellectual. At sometime in your spiritual work you may have to face this. Courage often requires you to act with an open heart, expand your horizons, unlearn or relearn some prize concept while letting go of something familiar. Courage is also about adaptability, change and having a flexible mind.

Here are some examples of strength and courage:

1. During the process of integration, you will be making spiritual decisions and you will need to have courage to abide by them.
2. Staying in tune with fellow spiritual workers and/or service work, e.g. meditations, discussing projects, etc. Here, you might have to adjust your time and energy. Sacrifice might be needed.
3. Ignoring emotional and physical weaknesses, e.g. fatigue and tiredness that limits your service. If you have an idea, such as writing, lectures, webinars, etc. then make the effort to implement it.
4. It takes courage to make personal sacrifices and demonstrate to others who presently are in spiritual need, e.g. family, community. Your own personal affairs and nonessential activities have to temporarily be placed on hold.
5. It takes moral courage to tackle life's problems on behalf of others, and to place your own wishes as secondary. It also takes courage to stand up for "obvious truth".

In today's world of distorted facts and actions of selfishness for personal gain, this is critical.

## Words of Cheer

In the midst of adversity, be it mental, emotional or physical, being of good cheer helps you through all forms of adversity. For there is no true defeat of the human spirit or losing faith in your own divinity, that you cannot pull yourself out of.

Everyday when you align with your Soul, as your Teacher and Guide, it is the one who provides rich rewards when all seems lost. When pain and sadness come your way, learn to respond with an inner knowingness that "it too shall pass" and the light of wisdom  of the Soul will prevail. Be naught dissuaded by future sorrows or vague "imagings". Know that by maintaining an inner connection with the Soul, that "livingness" flows through you and touches others to enable them to also move forward.

When you renounce the desire of the material nature in favor of human need, your body of desire becomes transmuted into a mind of the higher intuition. Serving in this way, with no thought or consideration about your own future, will bring you to becoming the perfect Sever of the Higher Self. Learn to cultivate daily that performing "right" action and good response. With this mindset, no power on Earth can prevent you or hold you back from achieving your destined spiritual goals.

Learn to like _who you are and what you are becoming_. Successfully acknowledging this fact is at the _level of knowing_.

# Appendix A - Techniques for Working in Consciousness

The following techniques are presented as "mental" exercises. You will note that some of the techniques have similar steps. But In order for these exercises to be successful, you may have to repeat the steps. S*incerity is key.*

1. **'As If' technique:**

   Just as an actor is 'acting out' the role of a particular character, you too can embody and emulate a particular spiritual truism, e.g. Soul value, virtue, or principle. This technique uses the creative imagination to create a bridge between the lower and abstract minds. This is "right" thoughtform building.

   **Process:**

   If you want to emulate or bring forth a Soul value, such as harmlessness, cooperation, goodwill, simply tune into its essence. Meditate on, and act "as if" you are already embodying this energy. Success means you've created a memory, "groove in consciousness", and action in life to "become harmless."

2. **'Technique of Light'**

   This technique is to literally overcome the power of illusion (e.g. a distortion of the truth), or stuck energy in the mental or emotional body. This describes how the light of the Personality (lower mind), and the light of the Soul <u>merge together</u> to transform the energy of the illusion. It can also be used for re-patterning thoughtforms.

   **Process:**

   - In your mind, become the observer and see the emotion / illusion dispassionately as they are just energy to transform.

- Next, visualize in your mind the Soul's light combined with your personality, creating one powerful floodlight shining on the illusion. Note, you may have to do this a number of times to destroy a persistent and deep-rooted illusion. .

- This process brings the light of truth or knowledge, and dissipates the illusion.

**Note:** When the Soul's light is merged with the personality's, it embodies the pure light of truth coming from the plane of pure reason and compassion, i.e. the Buddhic Plane. This technique implies a sincere cooperation of your personality with the Soul.

### 3. Observer Guides Purification process

The primary purpose for becoming the Observer is to guide the purification process. As a mental exercise, it will bring you to an awareness about the distinctions between thoughts, emotions, desires, addictions, or any limiting aspects of the lower mind. You can also observe impressions, ideas and insights. For this work, you are observing and deciding on a course of action to take.

**Process:**

- As the Observer, it is best to employ dispassion and discrimination by not being attached to anything in consciousness. You are strictly observing.
- When negative energies (whether within or outside of you) come up, try to analyze it and determine its source.
- Decide on course of action, such as using the Technique of Light. See also technique "Overcoming Fear and Anger".
- Perhaps, your ideas can be entered in the spiritual journal.

## 4. Overcoming Fear and Anger

Fear happens to all of us, and can even be felt by high level initiates. It will only be overcome by bringing forth Soul awareness or Light. As fear and anger are powerful feelings, it is recommended to work from the mental plane by forcing out or replacing the energy by the dynamic power of substitution.

Note, this exercise is meant to be done in your own private space where *you are safe and out of harms way.*

**Process:**

- Become the Observer and separate yourself from the fearful feeling or situation, and willfully relax your physical and emotional bodies. Steady your breathing, concentrate, then invoke stillness in the mind thru concentration and permeate the entire personality with pure white light. This is a process of invoking the higher will for calming your lower bodies.

- Much like the Technique of Light, continue invoking the Souls light until you realize the fear is neutralized. At first, you may have to do this several times.

- Practice invoking the polar opposite, moving from hate to love; fear to calmness. This is a form of substitution.

- When feelings of evil abound, the presence of the Soul's light and feelings of love will dispel this energy with *truth and pure reason.*

- When you have the courage to face your anger or fear, practice dispassion and observe the energy for what it is. Then listen for impressions or ideas for change and transformation.

- If you feel emotionally reactive, such as with anger, try to trace the energy to its source, and learn to transform them into something more 'life giving'. Ask: *why am I so angery at "X"?*

- During meditation, thoughts and feelings will come up. As the Observer note the tenor or tone of the thoughts and ask yourself: *What are my feelings and motivations?* Sincerity is key.

### 5. Mental grounding of "Monkey-Mind" chatter:

If you have all sorts of 'monkey-mind' thoughts and anxieties, simply take your mind off your thoughts and focus on the breath for several minutes. Focus only on the breath and feel yourself breathing. A centering meditation can be as simple as focusing on a candle flame, the beauty of a flower, or a mandala. It can be used during the day by taking a moment to *center* one's mind.

Its primary function is to bring stillness and a knowingness to being centered within the Soul's love and light. This allows you to sense a *tension from the Soul.* Remember how the Soul connection feels and *know* it's always there.

### 6. Technique of Detachment

This technique is much the same as the Technique of Light, except its primary purpose is simply to quell the energies of maya, or the craving energies of the form nature and felt in the emotional body.

**Process:**

- In your mind, become the observer and see the energy of maya with dispassion and detachment.
- When the feelings or cravings come up, become *dispassionate* or *detached* from the energy. As the esotericist, you mentally have an understanding about what it is, and *know not* to engage it.

### 7. Practicing Harmlessness

Progressing on the path requires courage, knowledge, and the practice of harmlessness. Harmlessness is a mindset that should be cultivated often.

It is important to bring forth and hold this awareness in consciousness for all encounters with people and situations in your environment. This is a good exercise until you have a firm rhythm established.

It is recommended and instructive to study yourself and see how the different effects that both *harmfulness* and *harmlessness* have on others. This can be done during meditation, or an evening review by analyzing the following:

- Harmlessness in thought
  - o Attempting to be harmless will help to eliminate harmful states of consciousness.
  - o Harmlessness brings caution in judgment, reticence of speech, ability to refrain from impulsive action, and a demonstration of a non-critical spirit.
  - o Harmlessness is an attitude of one who lives consciously as a Soul, whose natural inclination is love, and whose method is inclusiveness.
- Harmlessness in emotional reaction and action
  - o Study your emotional effects on others, so there is no mood, depression, nor emotional reaction that can harm to your fellow man. Violent aspiration, misplaced, or misdirected energy may harm others.
  - o The spiritual journal can also be a means for observing the effects of a harmful attitude, by studying the effects that anger and fear have on your consciousness.
  - o If you are harmless in your actions, remember how this looks and feels.

### 8. Use of Affirmations, Mantrams, Chanting

- Affirmations can affirm a certain principle, or idea. For example:

*"Each life crisis can lead to extended vision or to a separating wall".* OR *"The will to power must be galvanized by love".*

The affirmation can be used at a certain place in the meditation, or as a standalone. Using it either way, it is recommended to say the affirmation until the meaning is fully grasped. Then become silent and contemplate its deeper meaning. Allow your mind to become quiet, free of thoughts, and await impression from the Soul.

- Mantrams or chanting can function as focused sounds to help break up stuck energies.
  - For example, sounding OM will help to bring calmness to your thoughts and emotions.
  - Making a focused *'Eeee'* sound can be intense, and can break up a stuck energy, particularly in the emotional or mental body
  - *"Om mani padme hum "* – *"Praise to the Jewel in the Lotus."*
    This is said as an affirmation or statement to oneself or someone else for transforming one's body, speech, and mind into the higher consciousness.

Examples of Mantrams, Seed Thoughts, or Affirmations from *Alice A. Bailey - "Discipleship in the New Age, Vol. I":*

- *"With Self-Forgetfulness I Gather What I Need For The Helping of My Fellowmen".*

- *"With Self-Forgetfulness, I Breathe Out Love To My Fellow-Men".*

- *"Each life crisis can lead to extended vision or to a separating wall".*

**Affirmation of Love mantram**

*In the center of all Love I stand. From that center I, the soul, will outward move. From that center I, the one who serves, will work.*

*"May the love of the divine Self be shed abroad, in my heart, through my group, and throughout the world".*

➡ KNOW, that when <u>consciously using</u> these techniques, you are <u>expressing and embodying</u> the higher energies of the Soul.

# Appendix B - Stages of Discipleship

The Path of Discipleship is a subject that should be discussed in parallel with initiation as both subjects are deeply interconnected, and both directly deal with expansions of consciousness. The Path can be likened to a treadmill of sorts that moves in one forward direction towards ever expanding levels of awareness. From an esoteric point of view, it begins with the aspirant as the *one whom aspires* to higher spiritual goals, such as through the expression of compassion.

The aspirant's spiritual work will take him from the Mystical Path onto the Probationary Path where he will begin to build higher spiritual principles into his character and develop a higher aspirational life. Later, the aspirant becomes the disciple when he takes the path more seriously and transforms his inner self by integrating the energies of the Spiritual Triad, via the Soul.

The 6 Stages of Discipleship as defined by Alice A. Bailey and the Tibetan Master D.K. are:

| Discipleship Stage | Description of Phases |
| --- | --- |
| **Stage 1**<br><br>**'Little Chelaship'** | The aspirant develops his aspirational life towards the Soul, as the Soul also has a downward gaze on the aspirant.<br><br>Enters onto the Probationary Path.<br><br>Begins to practice Soul values, e.g. harmlessness, while integrating and developing character.<br><br>Esoteric inquiry and spiritual study drives the disciple to *want to know* and understand the changes he is beginning to sense within. He may go from teaching or teacher to another. |

| Stage 2 'Chela in the Light' | The Soul or senior disciple helps the aspirant to discover subtleties of shifts in consciousness. |
| --- | --- |
| | Building of the Antakarana begins for connecting to the Spiritual Triad and Ashram. |
| | Early recognition of the intuition indicates buddhic substance is replacing lower emotional energy. |
| | He begins to mentally *study* how the emotional body works and realizes that in order to control the emotional body, it must be done from the mental plane. This is an awareness of working on karma and glamours through purification. |
| | Since the disciple has progressed far enough to sense impressions from Soul, he has developed his *consciousness* and *livingness* threads through the partially built Antakarana. |
| | Disciple understands the difference between loving, and the *will to love*. This is akin to connecting the heart and mind together. |
| | With a shift from an emotional polarization in the astral plane to the mental plane, he takes 1st Initiation. |
| Stage 3 'Accepted Discipleship' | The disciple can easily invoke the light of the Soul and the light /intelligence of the Spiritual Triad. |
| | After having contacted the Master through a dream or impression, he has a stronger sense of responsibility and seriousness for carrying out Soul's and Master's wishes. Here he is possibly consciously connected with one of the 7 Ashrams for carrying out the Master's and Group work. |
| | He learns to *hold the point of tension* with the Soul and knows he meaning of *"holding the mind steady in the light"*. This is done through an act of will. |

|  | By mastering his emotional tendencies and nature, this helps to create a stability that makes the 2nd Initiation possible. This is akin to knowing who he is spiritually. |
|---|---|
| **Stage 4**<br><br>**'Chela on the Thread'** | Beginning with this stage, the disciple will have taken the 2nd Initiation.<br><br>The *thread* refers to the Ashram who is drawing the disciple closer for higher spiritual work. The disciple becomes *trusted* in the eyes of the Master and Ashram.<br><br>He identifies with *beingness* and can easily relate to energies of the Buddhic Plane. His personality is decentralized and acts with impersonality and indifference.<br><br>At end of this stage, the disciple takes the Third Initiation, and becomes "Monad-infused. He now has full identification with the Monad and his Ashram. He sees the Plan for the first time. The Soul is no longer the prime motivator for change. |
| **Stage 5**<br><br>**'Chela within the Aura'** | The disciple's tests and challenges in life are related to the work of Humanity and the Master's Ashram, rather than from his own personal life.<br><br>As the disciple-Initiate is aligned with the Master's and Ashram's aura, he can project his consciousness and etheric force directly onto the physical plane.<br><br>The disciple realizes the difference between *becoming and being*. This is an acknowledgment of full conscious awareness of the Monad. He is now approaching Arhat level as his consciousness now exists in the Spiritual Triad.<br><br>At the end of this stage he takes the 4<sup>th</sup> Initiation. His Soul and causal body are destroyed and his cycle of rebirth on the Earth plane is complete. |

| | |
|---|---|
| | |
| **Stage 6** <br> **'Chela within the Master's Heart'** | Initiate as Monad is fully identified as being the source of life aspect. <br><br> The initiate graduates to becoming a Master of the 5th degree. <br><br> As Master, he can can now build a m*ayavirupa*, or body of manifestation, and interact with the lower dense planes at will. <br><br> The Master is recognized by fellow Masters and can freely work in the planetary heart center and with the work of the Christ and/or Ashram. |

# Appendix C – Attributes, Virtues and Glamours of the 7 Rays

A study of the Rays is useful for disciples in determining the Soul and Personality rays.

- For the Soul ray, ask *"in my life what am I trending towards in how I feel or believe?"*

- For the personality ray, ask *"what vocation or activities am I inclined towards?"*

By studying the weaknesses (glamours) and virtues (strengths) of each of the rays, you can gain insight into your own psychology and how you approach life.

➡ Note: The following list originates from a 7 Ray Seminar by the 7 Ray Institute.

### Ray 1....Energy of Will or Power

People on this ray are motivated by a strong will often for either love or evil; for good they will be under the control selfless love and practice of wisdom whereas evil can be cruel and hard in nature. These people are natural leaders but they are people with strong feelings and minds.

The 1st Ray is currently "out of manifestation, but presence felt when stage of discipleship is reached."

Vices or Weaknesses or Weaknesses:

- Dynamic one-pointedness in mental or feeling nature.

- Destructive energy.

- Power realized selfishly

- A longing for power and authority: i.e. ambition without caring who gets hurt.

- Desire to dominate and control others.

- Pride, arrogance, intolerance, willfulness.

- Virtues or Strengths:

- Strength, courage, truthfulness, fearlessness, ability to grasp a great truth in a large minded way (e.g. politicians)

- Expressed strength and self-will, leading to a dynamic use of energy for the furtherance of the Plan.

- The use of destructive forces in order to prepare the way for re-building.

- The will to power in order to cooperate.

Glamours of Ray 1

- The glamour of physical strength.

- The glamour of personal magnetism or "the one at the center".

- The glamour of self-centeredness and personal potency.

- The glamour of selfish personal ambition.

- The glamour of selfish destiny, of the divine right of kings personally exacted.

- The glamour of destruction.

- The glamour of the superimposed will upon individuals and groups as dictator or ruler.

## Ray 2....Energy of Love - Wisdom

This ray has been out of cycle, but is returning for the next 2200 years. Ray 2 is led by Wisdom and people on this ray are those seeking pure knowledge or truth.

With the power of love present, the person can be a great teacher, e.g. in schools, ambassadors.

He has ability to grasp a "true' view on things, such as on world affairs or seeing the big picture of an issue. The individual on this ray will be in sincere and probably following a the spiritual path.

This Individual will study intellectual material and emotionally embrace a teaching on a specific subject. This will help to bring forth the intuition and true wisdom.

Vices or Weaknesses:

- Over absorption in study, coldness and indifference to others; contempt of mental limitation sensed in others.

- The power to build for selfish ends.

- Capacity to sense the Whole and to remain apart.

- The cultivation of a separative spirit.

- The realization of selfish desire.

- Longing for material well-being.

**Virtues or Strengths:**

- Inclusiveness.

- A longing for wisdom and truth.

- Sensitivity to the Whole.

- Renunciation of the great heresy of separtiveness.

- The revelation of the light.

- True illumination.

- Right speech through generated wisdom.

Glamours of Ray 2

- The glamour of the love of being loved.

- The glamour of popularity.

- The glamour of personal wisdom.

- The glamour of selfish responsibility.
- The glamour of self-pity, a basic glamour of this ray.
- The glamour of fear, based on undue sensitivity.
- The glamour of self-sacrifice or selfish service.

## Ray 3.....Energy of Active Intelligence

Ray 3 stimulates man's intellectual development and results in a marked increase of creative work.

This is the ray of the abstract thinker like a philosopher; this person can take an essence of truth make connections and see a wider view of a problem; this person will make a good businessman, be full of ideas but often to impractical to carry them out;

Working also with the 5th Ray, this person will make a great mathematician who can reach great abstract heights and bring practical uses into the scientific realm.

Vices or Weaknesses:

- Force manipulation through selfish desire.
- Intelligent use of force with wrong motive.
- Intense material and mental activity.
- The realization of energy as an end in itself.
- Longing for glory, beauty and for material objectives.
- Intellectual pride; coldness; inaccuracy to details; selfishness; overly critical of others.

Virtues or Strengths:

- Capacity for concentration on philosophic studies, patience
- The manipulation of energy in order to reveal beauty and truth.

- Adherence to right action by using of forces intelligently for the furtherance of the Plan.

- Ordered rhythmic activity in cooperation with the Whole.

- Desire for right revelation of divinity and light.

Glamours of Ray 3

- The glamour of being busy.

- The glamour of cooperation with the Plan in an individual and not a group way.

- The glamour of active scheming.

- The glamour of creative work—without true motive.

- The glamour of good intentions, which are basically selfish.

- The glamour of devious and continuous manipulation.

- The glamour of self-importance, from the standpoint of knowing.

## Ray 4....The Ray of Harmony through Conflict

Since 1924 and peaking early in 21$^{st}$ century, approximately 2025. It leads many on the path of discipleship and presents opportunity for the aspirant or disciple to work in combination with an ordained synthesis (or a combination of seemingly conflicting energies).

On this ray, the balance between inertia and activity is proportionally equal thus a conflict; this person love the path of least resistance and lets things to until tomorrow yet the urge to complete something is fast furious; This person is typically the artist or author who is very dramatic, showy, picturesque and often pessimistic or moody. These perpetual conflicting forces cause constant unease in the personality.

This type of person will be an excellent conversationalist but just a quickly withdraws into a mood.

Vices or Weaknesses:

- This person lacks moral courage, self-centered, extravagant and given to worries
- Confused tension within self.
- The darkness which precedes form expression.
- The veiling of the intuition because of internal conflict.

Virtues or Strengths:

- Generosity, sympathy, strong affections and devotion, quickness of perception and physical courage
- Identification with humanity, the fourth Creative Hierarchy.
- Abnormal sensitivity to that which is the Not Self.
- He is immersed in constant points of crisis, leading to unity and harmony.
- The evocation of the intuition, right judgment and pure reason.

Glamours of Ray 4

- The glamour of harmony, aiming at personal comfort and satisfaction.
- The glamour of war.
- The glamour of conflict, with the objective of imposing righteousness and peace.
- The glamour of vague artistic perception.
- The glamour of psychic perception instead of intuition.

**Ray 5....The Ray of Concrete Science or Knowledge**

Concrete knowledge, science and basic quality of discrimination; The 5$^{th}$ Ray in combination with the 3$^{rd}$ ray provides any further mental intensification necessary for discovery.

Ray 5 influences and produces stimulation in man which lies behind the scientific approach to truth in all departments of human thought. The 5$^{th}$ ray also describes the general theory of education, and how to convey concrete knowledge in an effective way.

Vices or Weaknesses:

- Narrow-mindedness, harsh criticism, prejudice, lack of sympathy and reverence, arrogance and egotism.

- The energy of ignorance.

- The power to rationalize and destroy.

- Mental separation.

- Desire for knowledge. This leads to material activity.

- Detailed analysis of the individual and ignoring the whole.

- Intense materialism and temporarily the negation of Deity.

- Intensification of the power to isolate.

- The implications of wrong emphasis.

- Distorted views of truth.

Virtues or Strengths:

- Strong capacity for accurate statements,

- Justice, perseverance, common sense, uprightness, independence and keen intellect

- Mental devotion to form and form activity.

- Theology, leading to a knowledge of reality.

- The realization of the soul and its potentialities.

- Sensitivity to the Higher Self, to light and to wisdom.

- Spiritual and mental devotion.

- The knowledge and power to take initiation. Individual has knowledge of the initiation process and can have the ability to apply a sensed synthesis of energies.

Glamours of Ray 5

- The glamour of materiality, or over-emphasis of form.

- The glamour of the intellect.

- The glamour of knowledge and of definition.

- The glamour of assurance, based on a narrow point of view.

- The glamour of the outer, which hides the inner form.

**Ray 6....Abstract Idealism and Devotion**

Ray of devotion or idealism and basic quality is devoted *sensitivity* to an ideal.

A person on this ray is full of religious devotion; Can lay down their lives for an ideal but will not help someone else not with their sympathies;

Can make great orators or religious leaders but not good statesmen. Their way of spiritual work is through devotion with the desire of making a connection with the Higher Self.

Vices or Weaknesses:

- Selfish and jealous love, partiality, prejudice, intolerance of other views

- Violence. Fanaticism. Willful adherence to an ideal.

- Short sighted blindness.

- Militarism and a tendency to make trouble with others and with groups.

- The power to see no point except one's own.

Virtues or Strengths:

- Devotion, love, loyalty and tenderness and reverence, strong devotion to an ideal, especially to a "personal" God such as in religion

- Rapid reaction to glamour and illusion.

- Emotional devotion and bewildered idealism.

- Intense capacity to be personal and emphasize personalities, which leads to focused idealism.

- Reaction to, and sympathy with, the point of view of others.

- Willingness to see the work of other people progress along their chosen lines.

- Peace and not war; The good of the Whole and not the part.

Glamours of Ray 6

- The glamour of devotion and idealism, often leading to fanaticism.

- The glamour of adherence to forms and persons.

- The glamour of loyalties, of creeds.

- The glamour of emotional response.

- The glamour of sentimentality.

- The glamour of World Saviors and Teachers.

- The glamour of the narrow vision.

**Ray 7....Order and Ceremonial Magic**

This person will delight in doing things in order, almost like a rhythm or ritual and according to rule and precedent; ray of the high priest and the perfection of an organization working in harmony with all its parts; the ray of creating the perfect form such as a sculptor, architect or designer of beautiful forms

This is the Ray of creating the divine in form such as a sculptor, architect or designer of beautiful forms.

The service of helping others transform their highest dreams into accomplished realities through structured organization.

Vices or Weaknesses:

- Superstitious, bigoted, formalism, narrowness, superficial judgment.

- Black magic, or the use of magical powers for selfish ends.

- The power to "sit upon the fence" till the selfish values emerge.

- Disorder and chaos, through misunderstanding of the Plan.

- The wrong use of speech to bring about chosen objectives, i.e. telling an untruth.

- Sex magic. The selfish perversion of soul powers, such as promiscuity.

- Rightly applied, this Ray will lead the disciple on the path of practicing White magic and the use of Soul powers for spiritual ends.

Virtues or Strengths:

- The identification of oneself with reality or the whole, e.g. an organization

- Right order through right magic – right use of force and energy for creating symmetry;

- Power to cooperate with the Whole.

- Understanding of the Plan.

- The magical work of interpretation.

Glamours of Ray 7

- The glamour of the relation of the opposites.

- The glamour of that which brings together and constitutes the group.

- The glamour of the physical body.

- The glamour of the mysterious and the secret.

- The glamour of sex magic.

- The glamour of the emerging manifested forces from a group or individual, i.e. and manipulating them.

# Glossary and Definitions

| Term | Definition |
|------|------------|
| Abstract Mind | See 'Mind' for definition. |
| Antakarana | There is a gap in consciousness existing between the personality and the Spiritual Triad. This gap is a type of break of "unrefined matter" between mental permanent atom of the Spiritual Triad, and the mental unit of the lower mind. The Tibetan Master, Djwhal Kuhl tells us *"when the disciple is beginning to be focused on mental levels...,"* he begins to build the Antakarana. Ultimately, for the individual a bridge will connect our regular waking consciousness with our pure Spirit, the Monad. <br><br> The Antakarana, also called the Rainbow Bridge is a thread of mental substance that identifies with consciousness and not with form. There are several threads that make up one single whole. It is the personality that builds the creative thread. The "consciousness thread" as it is esoterically known, is anchored in the head and projected by the Soul. The "life thread" is anchored in the heart and projected by the Spirit or Monad. As a whole, the Antakarana is a symbol of living form created by the power of thought projected from the personality to the Spiritual Triad. Its main function is to link the brain with the lowest aspect of Manas of the Spiritual Triad. As a result, the Antakarana functions as a bridge connecting the higher and the lower aspects of our minds. |
| Ashram | Sanskrit: a monastic community, or other place of religious instruction. An ashram is the center where the Master gathers the disciples and aspirants for personal instruction. It is seen as a center of influence or inclusion where energies emanate from the Master outward to the periphery. This circulation |

|  | of energy connects the Masters with his disciples, and provides instruction and feedback via telepathy. |
|  | The Ageless Wisdom tells us there are seven main ashrams and 49 subsidiary ashrams, some of which have yet to be formed. Each ashram is a center around which disciples and Spiritual workers gather for personal teaching from a Master. The Master works with the group to focus a particular energy for carrying out the Plan. |
|  | While part of the Ashram, disciples are taught to use the power of thought to focus the conscious mind. The disciple works with the Soul as he invokes the intuition. If the disciple is successful, he will bring forth illumination, Soul impulse, and intuitive perception. His mental orientation will enable him to effectively work in outer plane groups and help in manifesting the Plan. |
| **Aspect** | Aspect refers to the three aspects of God that have been revealed to mankind by Shamballa. The Shamballic energy is stepped down to Hierarchy: <br><br> • 1st Aspect - Will <br><br> • 2nd Aspect - Love-wisdom <br><br> • 3rd Aspect - Active Intelligence |
| **Aspirant** | This term describes the spiritual seeker who is on the Probationary Path or the initial stages of "conscious" spiritual growth. He is one who consciously 'aspires', is purifying the lower personality nature, and looks for acceptance to the spiritual path. |
| **Astral Plane** | The Astral Plane is the plane where the individual experiences emotional sensitivities. <br><br> It is characterized by the energy of desire. For the majority of humanity it is a plane of a distorted depiction of reality. It is composed of a conglomeration of interacting emotional energies |

| | |
|---|---|
| | and conditions the everyday person's astral-emotional body. Until he can learn to bring balance and stability from these forces and energies in his own astral-emotional body, he will continue to be a victim to its power. |
| **'At-onement'** | The whole of man's evolution of the human spirit is a series of progressive unification of the personality in relation to the Soul, then later with the Monad.<br><br>At-one-ment occurs on all levels: emotional, intuitional, spiritual and Divine levels through the man's inner fire. The burning proceeds through the destruction of all forms that create a barrier. This includes burning away anything that inhibits communication between the mental, emotional or etheric bodies.<br><br>This eventually results in the Personality's bodies functioning as one and facilitating the Soul integrated Personality. |
| **Awareness** | Awareness is that quality where the mind is 'conscious' of what it is observing in its space, e.g. registering impressions from the abstract mind, or for identifying glamours or illusions.<br><br>Awareness also infers a level of 'knowingness'. As the observer, you come to the realization that *"you are the one who is observing"*, and are consciously aware of this fact. It is another word for consciousness. |
| **Atma-Buddhi-Manas** | These three energies are extensions of the pure Spirit, the Monad, and make up the Spiritual Triad. Each represents the three aspects of the Divine:<br><br>• Atma – Universal Spirit represented by the 1st Aspect, i.e. the Will<br>• Buddhi – represented by the 2nd Aspect, i.e. Divine love, pure reason, non-duality, intuition and serenity; vehicle of the Atma |

| | |
|---|---|
| | • Manas – represented by the 3rd Aspect, i.e. Intelligence. Manas is the highest aspect of the Mental Plane. After the Soul-integrated personality begins to create the Antakarana, it is the first means of contact with the Spiritual Triad. |
| **Buddhic Plane / Buddhi** | Sanskrit: to enlighten, perceive, awaken or cognize or understand. Buddhi is the principle or organ in man which give him spiritual consciousness and is the vehicle of the most high part of man – the Atman – the faculty which manifests as understanding, judgement, discrimination and cognition. Buddhi is that energy characteristic of the Buddhic plane. Man's ordinary consciousness in life in his present stage of evolution is almost wholly kama-manas or of desire / emotional nature, that is driven by or thinking with his emotional-desire body. On the path of liberation, it is a major goal in the Soul's evolution to replace all energies of the lower personality expression with its higher correspondence. When the individual makes the effort to raise his consciousness connect with the Plane of the Intuition, the Soul facilitates the flow of Buddhi to replace the lower kama-manas. Buddhi represents the 2nd aspect of the Spiritual Triad. It is characterized by Divine love, pure reason, non-duality, intuition and serenity. After the process of building the Antakarana has begun, the personality can begin making contact with the Buddhic Plane. During the paths of Probation and Discipleship, the disciple will begin replacing his lower astral energies with Buddhi. Meditation is one of the prime means for contacting the Buddhic Plane, and drawing forth the intuition. |
| **Causal Body** | The causal body is the body of the Soul and a storehouse of wisdom accumulated from previous incarnations. Composed of buddhi and manas, it stores wisdom and "acts of goodness". It also stores negative and selfish acts accumulated through all |

| | |
|---|---|
| | the Soul's incarnations extending over hundreds of lifetimes. Over this long journey, the Soul's purpose is to incarnate lifetime after lifetime to ultimately cleanse and purify the causal body. |
| **Chakras (or Energy Centers)** | See 'etheric body' for definition. |
| **Christ or "Christ-like"** | The Christ, or "Christos" (Greek for the 'Anointed One') refers to a high state of consciousness, and not just the man. Jesus the man was a separate initiate on his own path of liberation. During that life 2000 years ago, he took the Fourth Initiation and merged his consciousness with the Christ consciousness and "at-oned" becoming "Christ-Jesus" or "Jesus the Christ". This initiation was significant for mankind, as the Christ became the first human to fully embrace and practice "love-wisdom" in consciousness. This involved ensconcing atomic matter from the Spiritual Triad with "love-wisdom" on all the planes and subplanes, of the Cosmic "energetic" physical plane. |
| | When we use the term 'Christ-like', we mean that we are expressing virtues, e.g. kindness, goodwill, cooperation, and love as the Christ practiced, and taught. |
| | On the spiritual path, Service Workers or disciples aspire to become 'Christ-like' and evolve their consciousness accordingly towards the expression of love and goodwill. With this focus, our mental (thoughts), emotions (feelings) are purified and transformed as we engage in service. |
| **Christ Principle** | The Christ Principle indicates the illusive but potent energy of the Christ within an individual. |
| | This energy is not limited to the Christ but is always part of the Soul, and can be accessed by aligning with the Soul and expressing its values, such as |

| | |
|---|---|
| | selfless love. For one who holds this alignment, he has become a living embodiment of this energy and exhibiting all its qualities. This is, in effect an identification with this type of energy, while exhibiting all of its qualities.<br><br>The main characteristics of the Christ-principle is selfless love, evoking the spirit of understanding, goodwill and cooperation. For most people, it is expressed as an urge towards better human relationships. |
| **Concrete Mind** | See 'Mind' for definition. |
| **Conscious Awareness** | Conscious awareness generally refers to an action, or state of being 'conscious' or 'aware' of something, someone or a situation.<br><br>This denotes the mind is what the Service Worker wants to develop so it can become a useful tool for observation of various energies, e.g. thoughts, impressions, and forces in his consciousness. |
| **Consciousness** | Consciousness is the relationship between spirit and matter. The principle of consciousness involves a person's spiritual awakening and his evolutionary progress through physical expression. Using his consciousness, man 'understands' and finds relationship between physical appearance and the subjective world of Reality.<br><br>When individualization took place millions of years ago, man made a transition from the animal to the human kingdom. This resulted in a major step in human evolution, when man evolved to having self-consciousness with a separate personality. The very reason behind man's existence is for the progressive unfoldment of his consciousness to eventually achieve full conscious awareness on all planes. These unfoldments, esoterically speaking, are known as 'initiations' and are attainments of when man's consciousness and awareness is |

| | |
|---|---|
| | expanded into new realizations of reality. With the passage of time, he developed his consciousness to be aware of his separative existence, leading to his spiritual understanding and relationship with the Soul. This finally leads to group identification. |
| | A finer point to grasp is that man's consciousness, and its development is not just associated with his physical incarnation. Man's consciousness is associated with the Soul , so it does not matter whether he is in or out of incarnation. |
| | His consciousness persists. |
| | It's a fact that the consciousness can evolve much easier if there are no limitations from the physical plane, e.g. the untrained human brain. |
| | A finer point to grasp is that man's consciousness, and its development is not just associated with his physical incarnation. Man's consciousness is associated with the Soul , so it does not matter whether he is in or out of incarnation. His consciousness persists. It's a fact that the consciousness can evolve much easier if there are no limitations from the physical plane, e.g. the untrained human brain. |
| **Continuity of Consciousness** | A major goal for the meditator is to establish a continuity of consciousness for perceiving the higher levels of mind, and allow for a continual flow of impressions from the Spiritual Triad. The full expression of this process  will most likely not happen until the Third Initiation. 'Continuity' refers to the disciple being able to successfully hold the 'tension of connection' over a period of time. This connection will lead to the more advanced stages of discipleship and initiation for creating a "continuity of consciousness". |
| | Through sustained esoteric meditation, the gap between the lower bodies and the higher mind of the Soul will be bridged. This will result in a soul- |

| | |
|---|---|
| | infused personality When enough of the "Bridge of Light or Antakarana has been built, this process will facilitate a 'continuity of consciousness'. |
| **Cosmic "energetic" physical plane** | The Cosmic "energetic" physical plane encompasses 7 planes of human experience, each with its own 7 subplanes. In all, there are 49 planes. The first four are formless, whereas the last three are more dense, and with form.<br><br>A long-term goal of the spiritual seeker is to ultimately become a Master of the Wisdom where he has total conscious awareness on all 7 planes. The seven planes are:<br>1. The Divine Space<br>2. The Monadic<br>3. The Atmic<br>4. The Buddhic Plane<br>5. The Mental plane<br>6. The Astral plane<br>7. The dense physical, plus the etheric planes |
| **Crisis** | For the esotericist, crisis represents an opportunity for spiritual evolution in consciousness for transforming glamour, illusions or attachments. On the spiritual path, crisis can also be seen as an opportunity to either stay where you're at and not progress, grow, or embrace a new orientation and paradigm in consciousness.<br>For the disciple, it is the handling of a crisis as to how much he extends his vision and thereby allows "fresh knowledge to flow". |
| **Desire, Energy of** | Desire is the lowest form of will. As an esotericist, you will want to train yourself to become the observer for learning to differentiate between desire and emotion.<br>The fundamental differences are:<br>• 'Desires' characterize a wanting or grasping feeling. These are astral or emotional feelings stimulated by lower mental thoughts, which |

|  | entered the astral-emotional body. |
|---|---|
|  | • 'Emotion' is the relationship between thought and feeling. When a person feels and thinks about a feeling, then the reaction is felt in the astral-emotional body. Thus, emotion is created. |
| **Detachment** | An important esoteric trait to cultivate, involves being able to stand back from a situation with dispassion and with an impersonal viewpoint.<br><br>This will allow the Service Worker to become the 'intelligent' observer by looking at a situation from a different perspective, and by moving from the awareness of the personality to that of the Soul. |
| **D.K.** | D.K. is an abbreviation for Djwhal Kuhl, also known as "The Tibetan Master". He is an Initiate of the 5th Degree or Spiritual Master who worked with Alice A. Bailey from 1919 – 1949. As an amanuensis, Bailey wrote 24 books on numerous esoteric topics of the Ageless Wisdom, dictated telepathically by the Tibetan.<br><br>During their 30-year collaboration, Master D.K. is said to be the primary means of communication for the Ancient Wisdom of the Spiritual Hierarchy.<br><br>Alice A. Bailey wrote that D.K.'s intention was to further the revelation of the esoteric teachings on teaching and training spiritual aspirants in the 20th and 21st Centuries. Other significant works transmitted were on understanding the nature of right human relations, group work, power of goodwill, and to prepare humanity for the Externalization of the Hierarchy and the Reappearance of the Christ. |
| **Disciple and Discipleship** | A disciple is a person who has undergone a considerable purification in his personality and is pledged to serve humanity and cooperate with the Plan. He knows he stands at the midway point between the seductions of the 'old ways' of the form |

|  | |
|---|---|
|  | nature, and resonating to the relatively new Soul awareness, which is day-by-day dominating his consciousness.<br><br>The disciple as an occultist is a person that studies the effects of energy and force, and integrates the information for the benefit of whatever group he is associated with. He is conscious of his own innate powers as he seeks to let the Soul direct his consciousness. Therefore, he has a sense of responsibility of the "Soul-force" that motivates him, and radiates from his personality.<br><br>His primary purpose is three-fold:<br>1. He is dedicated towards serving humanity through group work.<br>2. He will cooperate and implement the Plan as best he understands it through his contact with the Soul, as he sees himself as an outpost for the work of the Master.<br>3. On a personal level, he seeks to establish a new rhythm of continual Soul contact by learning to function on the higher planes of the Spiritual Triad, and release any attachments to the lower planes. |
| **Discrimination** | As you advance on the spiritual path, you will learn to distinguish between the different energies (thoughts) and forces (expressions of Will) in your outer surroundings, or consciousness. This is the ability to step back, examine, analyze, and observe a situation using the finite ego.<br><br>With this ability you will be able to decide on the 'right' course of action to take. You will learn to make conscious choices between the pairs of opposites, for example: right vs. wrong, or appropriate vs. inappropriate, real from the unreal, etc.<br>When the Spiritual employs discrimination, he may ask: *"Do I see this situation in stark terms, or are* |

| | |
|---|---|
| | *there shades of gray?"*<br><br>In this example, you may have to bring forth the intuition. |
| **Energy** | Energy refers to those things, e.g. thoughts, feelings and sensations that are 'energized'. For an Esotericist, he will be interested in how energy exists in consciousness and conditions reality.<br><br>As he observes the energy, he asks:<br><br>• "What is its nature and characteristics?"<br><br>• "How does it aid or hinder me in my spiritual work?" |
| **Esoteric and Esotericist** | The term 'esoteric' refers to those perceptions, which are not typically recognized in the life of the everyday man. It can be broadly described as stages of awareness for the Service Worker, and later disciple.<br><br>The esotericist is *consciously* aware of the forces and energies in his environment. His awareness is extended to the mental level, in contrast to the mystic who feels. His task is to determine how he can control, and direct the energies for the benefit of humanity.<br><br>The path of the esotericist is one of the intellect and knowledge. His is a mental approach and he knows that true understanding of the energies and forces that shape the world, are a product of the blending of the intellect, love and devotion. The result is wisdom in action.<br><br>The esotericist will be:<br>1. On the probationary path and continuing onto the path of Discipleship. The Service Worker begins to register ideas, concepts and principles in the abstract mind. He is beginning his observations about energy and force, while |

| | during this time, an awareness of his subjective life is developing. |
|---|---|
| | 2. This is brought about by establishing connections with the Soul. He is learning to recognize the energies in his environment and make connections to those activities occurring in the etheric world. |
| | 3. In the intermediate stages, he will experience insights in his consciousness where the light of the Soul is perceived through impression and the intuition. At this point, the esotericist is making a connection with the Buddhic Plane. |
| | 4. In the advanced stages, the disciple-esotericist begins to 'consciously' build the Antakarana. His mind is completely reoriented so he recognizes the Plan, and begins to dimly sense the nature of the Will and its "right" expression. |
| **Esoteric Sense** | The term "esoteric sense" denotes a gradually developing spiritual power in the disciple, who is strongly at-one and aligned with the Soul. This power allows him to live and function subjectively on mental levels and lower 18 subplanes. The esoteric sense allows him to: <br>• Live and function subjectively in the mind. The person holds an attitude, which can orient in both the inner and outer planes. <br>• Possess a constant inner contact with the Soul. This marks a transcendence of personality concentration. <br>• Actively demonstrates love and wisdom in all he does. <br>• Mentally tune into the realms of thought and ideas. This allows him as a service worker to choose those mental concepts and ideals, which will be recognized in the world of everyday thinking, and living. |

| | |
|---|---|
| | • He will develop an attitude of mind where he will be able to orient himself in that high place of inspiration and light. There he will communicate with and discover his fellow-workers as they will work together in implementing divine intentions.<br><br>• To cultivate the esoteric sense, he knows meditation is required. As time passes, he realizes that his meditations have caused him to grow spiritually and enabled a strong spiritual orientation. This has resulted in him developing an attitude of the detached observer. |
| **Etheric Body** | The etheric body is the energy or 'vital' vehicle, which interpenetrates and corresponds to the dense physical body. It is a finer level of matter than the dense physical form, and has seven major chakras or energy centers, each of which gives us vitality, energy and life.<br><br>The chakras correspond approximately to the nervous system and ductless glands, which maintain our life processes.<br><br>The seven chakras are:<br><br>1. Base center<br><br>2. Sacral center<br><br>3. Solar Plexus<br><br>4. Heart<br><br>5. Throat<br><br>6. Ajna or 3rd eye<br><br>7. Crown<br>From the spiritual viewpoint, the etheric body is a focus for the pure Spirit, the Monad in the dense physical world. The centers are formed entirely of streams of force, pouring down from the Soul, that act as a conduit from the Monad. |

|  | They are connected with the Will aspect of the Monad, e.g. the will to live.<br><br>The etheric body receives and distributes force from many different directions, e.g. from prana, impressions from the abstract mind or Soul, psychic impressions or thoughts, and from others through telepathy. The centers are recognized as focal points of energy located in the etheric body, and have a definite use. They act as transmitters of certain forms of energy consciously directed by the Soul with the intent of driving the physical body to fulfilling the Soul's purpose. |
|---|---|
| **Force** | Esoterically, force is that energy which is projected by an individual or group with intent and motive. Often it is the energy of the will. The individual's motive may have positive or negative intent. This is in the initial stages of development. Later, he will come to learn that force and will are closely tied to the increasing influence of the Monad.<br><br>The esotericist will learn to use force for the benefit of the group in fulfillment of the Plan.<br>He will be consciously aware of the potential impact this focused force or energy has on others. |
| **Glamour** | Glamour is an illusion in the astral-emotional body, and is associated with emotional limitations in consciousness. It is overcome by a conscious 'mental' effort by both the personality, and the Soul as they shine the higher light of truth, and understanding on a particular illusionary energy.<br>It is the higher light from the Soul that transforms the illusion. |
| **Harmlessness** | Practiced harmlessness will orient the Spiritual worker's values towards developing an attitude of helping others, and training oneself not to act or say things of an impulsive or critical nature. On the other hand, a person with a 'harmful' attitude usually has a selfish, and ego-centric nature. |

In order to progress on the path, it is important to bring forth and hold this awareness in consciousness for all encounters with people and situations in your environment.

In the world today, harmlessness is demonstrated by a person with right motive, practiced goodwill, and has the ability to not engage in impulsive action or speech. The use of harmlessness in action and speech goes a long way towards fostering openness to communication, trust and understanding.

It is recommended and instructive to study one's own consciousness and see how the different effects that both *harmfulness* and *harmlessness* have on others. This can be done during meditation, or an evening review by analyzing the following:

- Harmlessness in thought

  o Attempting to be harmless will help to eliminate harmful states of consciousness.

  o Harmlessness brings caution in judgment, reticence of speech, ability to refrain from impulsive action, and a demonstration of a non-critical spirit.

  o Harmlessness is an attitude of one who lives consciously as a Soul, whose natural inclination is love, and whose method is inclusiveness.

- Harmlessness in emotional reaction

  o Study your emotional effects on others, so there is no mood, depression, nor emotional reaction that can harm your fellow man. Violent aspiration, misplaced, or misdirected energy may harm others, so look not only at your wrong tendencies, but at the use of your virtues.

  o The spiritual journal can also be a means for observing the effects of a harmful

| | |
|---|---|
| | attitude, by studying the effects that anger and fear have on your consciousness.<br><br>• Harmlessness in Action<br><br>If the individual is harmless in his actions, it would be of great benefit to remember how this looks and feels. |
| **Hierarchy and Masters** | The Hierarchy is that group of beings that make up the kingdom of Souls. These elder beings are characterized by love and wisdom, acquired over millennia and lifetimes. At one time, they too had bodies and lives that wrestled with the dangers, sorrows, and pains of everyday living. As they struggled to master the physical, astral and mental planes and triumph over matter, they eventually became liberated Masters of the Wisdom.<br>This Hierarchy is made up of Chohans, Masters, Adepts, and initiates working through their disciples. As custodians of the Plan, their chief responsibilities are:<br><br>• Work constantly at the task of awakening the consciousness aspect in all forms.<br>• The Hierarchy only works through individuals and groups whose ideas and attitudes are inclusive, non-critical and non-separative. These people will typically be disciples, men and women of goodwill.<br>• The Hierarchy helps to direct world events through the free will of humanity by assisting the unfoldment of consciousness of the political, religious and economic world group forms. They do this by impressing those who are in contact with Them, through the inflow of ideas, and through revelation. |
| **Higher Mind** | The Higher Mind refers to the Soul and is the means for conveying illumination to the lower mind through alignment with the Soul.<br>The abstract mind is the highest level of the Mental |

| | |
|---|---|
| | Plane, and the lowest aspect of the Spiritual Triad. Therefore, it acts as a transmitter of spiritual energies by the Soul, e.g. the intuition or pure reason. It is the faculty that enables man to make contact with the Plan, and to register divine ideas, or to isolate a pure 'truth.'<br><br>With the construction of the Antakarana, the abstract mind is brought into conscious functioning. In addition, creative work is enhanced in the abstract mind through meditation, study, and service. Disciples and Spiritual workers should aim to train themselves in:<br><br>• Aligning with the higher mind and brain through studying and understanding the etheric body and the chakras.<br><br>• Establishing a synthesis in the personality by creating a bridge- connection between the following:<br>  o The brain and the mind, when aligned allows the Soul to express itself easier through the lesser man.<br>  o The lower mind, the Soul and higher mind when connected will help to allow for the flow of ideas and impressions from the Soul.<br><br>This 'bridging' process consists of focusing the consciousness into the next higher level of awareness, thereby facilitating the mind to progressively advance along the path of spiritual evolution. |
| **Higher Self** | Depending on the individual's stage of evolution, the spiritual seeker considers the Soul as the Higher Self, whereas the Initiate considers the Monad to be the Higher Self. H.P. Blavatsky defined the higher self as Atma "the inseparable ray of the Universe and one self". Its basic premise states that it is a being who is intelligent, omnipotent, conscious, and is one's real self.<br><br>An individual can make conscious contact with the Higher Self through the practice of meditation. |

| | |
|---|---|
| | Meditation allows the individual to achieve peace, salvation, enlightenment, or develop a more enlightened perspective into man's most intractable questions, such as the purpose of existence or death, etc. |
| **Hindrance** | A hindrance can be any action, thought, or feeling that prevents you from directly connecting with the pure nature of your Soul. It can also be an energy, e.g. a glamour or illusion that keeps you from knowing a higher truth, or practicing a virtue. Examples of Hindrances: Anger, fear, selfishness, attachment, worry, doubt, anxiety, laziness, lack of discipline, boredom, harmfulness, restlessness, carelessness, apathy, ill will and worry. |
| **Illusion** | Illusion is one of three main limitations in consciousness that the Spiritual worker must overcome in order to evolve, and move onto the path of discipleship and later, initiation. The other two limiting energies are glamour and maya. Illusion is associated with thought energy, e.g. seeing something in consciousness, but not in its true form. |
| **Impression** | Just as we say: "*I got the impression that.....*" or "*My first impression was....*", our Souls are using the very same mechanism for transmitting an impression. The term impression, is often associated with the following: inspiration, guidance, impulse, incentive, influence, and aspiration. It refers to the same idea of stimulation of energy or force. Impression by its very form is of a subjective nature, and is closely aligned with the intuition. Impressions often come in the form of symbols, or an image, and register in the finite ego as an idea, or thought. Impressions can also be felt in the etheric body, which acts as a sensitive receiver of impulses from other outside sources. Impressions will typically come from a number of sources: |

| | |
|---|---|
| | • Soul – this is the most common form of contact after alignment of the personality has been established.<br>• Master or Guide – this can be in the form of direct telepathic impression after the inner mechanism for sensitivity has been developed.<br>• Disciple's Group – this would be a telepathic interchange with members of a service group with whom he is collaborating. The member could be part of a physical group or communicating through subjective levels.<br>It is incumbent on the Spiritual worker to develop sensitivity to impulses from these sources to be an effective agent of service for the Soul and the Group. |
| **Impulse** | Impulse is a type of stimulation from the Soul, and is often associated with an impression, or the intuition. The esotericist may register the impulse as a thought in the finite ego, or perhaps he may receive stimulation in his etheric body. Either way, the impulse will motivate him or be moved to take action in an activity, e.g. his spiritual work or with a group. |
| **Initiation, The Path of** | Initiation is a process of penetrating into the mysteries of the science of the Self. The Ageless Wisdom teachings describe spiritual initiation as a process that centers around crisis, and when successfully completed, it represents a major step in evolution for the personality and Soul.<br><br>The process involves working directly with energies, forces, and reconciling the pairs of opposites.<br>Each of the major initiations is considered to be a rare event, and lifetimes can pass between each major shift. A shift represents a paradigm shift in consciousness, where the disciple fundamentally transforms an old way of being to the new way of thinking in consciousness. |

| | |
|---|---|
| | As much as the initiate' clears away blockages and senses energies from the higher planes, he will expand his consciousness. |
| **Intuition** | "Intuition is a blend of the two divine qualities of buddhi-manas, or intuitive spiritual understanding (involving interpretation and identification) and the higher abstract mind, which is essentially the power to comprehend that which is not concrete or tangible but which is, in reality, an innate recognition of the lower aspects of the divine Plan...Alice A. Bailey "Externalization of the Hierarchy". |
| | Intuition is a spiritual intelligence that culminates as the awareness of ideas and 'truths' emanating from the Buddhic Plane. It is registered in the finite ego, and appears as a thought, an impression, or a symbol in the mind. In this way, it is a form of 'direct knowledge.' It is only when the disciple shifts his consciousness onto the mental level, and his mind establishes an alignment with the Soul, that ideas may be registered and revealed. |
| | Intuition brings three qualities: |
| | 1 – **Illumination:** 'light' pours from the Buddhic Plane to illuminate the intellect of the mind. This is the light that 'Shows the Way.' |
| | 2 – **Understanding:** through the intuition, the integrated personality, with the aid of the Soul, has contact with life, about the group's purpose and plans. |
| | 3 – **Love:** with intuition from the Buddhic Plane where there is no separation or duality, love is present in a divine form. It negates all criticism, barriers and separation. |
| | The intuition enables man to become clearly aware of reality, e.g. insights or ideas about a person, group or situation. As the Service Worker and disciple progress on the path, he will learn to use the intuition as a tool for service, instead of relying |

| | |
|---|---|
| | only on the lower finite ego as the most trustworthy source for 'knowledge'. |
| **Integration** | On the Path of Return, the spiritual man gradually integrates the mental, emotional, and physical vehicles to form one whole, and ultimately work under the direction of the intelligent, conscious thinker, the Soul. When they are united in this way, the man functions as one living being.<br><br>The aspirant and later disciple learns to fuse, and align the three lower vehicles into one functioning whole, which is the personality. Integration and alignment with the Soul causes his mind to become reoriented towards serving in the wider community.<br><br>Just as the individual learns to integrate all his disparate parts together, mankind progressively is integrating the various parts of the family unit, the social order, the nation, world of nations, and humanity into a relational whole.<br><br>This integration is not just occurring on a physical level, but is an attitude of mind. Man's consciousness comes to recognize his relationship and interrelationship with all parts to the whole and how they work together. Later, his integration with the Buddhic Plane allows him to know truth directly, through the intuition. |
| **Invocation / Evocation** | Invocation / Evocation describes an appeal and urge towards the light by spiritually-minded humanity. It produces a pushing forward for expanding consciousness and moving into the realms of greater knowledge of Soul light and life. It is a process of appeal and response that brings the invoker into alignment with the Hierarchy and the Greater Life.<br><br>For the disciple-esotericist, it infers that *"an awareness of what's needed and desired is a driving understanding at the level of "knowing".* If he is mindful of the esoteric significance and of the |

| | |
|---|---|
| | dynamics of this process he can be most effective in his service activities as he intuits the idea then works towards concretizing it on the physical plane. Examples of higher evocation could be evoking the principle of sharing, bringing forth the thought of peace, eliminating violence and warring tendencies, upholding human rights, the cause of freedom, or caring for the environment. |
| **Knowingness** | Knowingness, or 'gnosis' refers to that place in consciousness where the Service Worker or disciple has a direct connection with the higher mind. Through this connection, he understands that 'knowing' happens directly, where not even a thought stands between his mind, and the thing he knows.<br><br>In the Ageless Wisdom teachings, knowingness is an important concept when the disciple wants to bring forth a 'truth,' or is reconciling the pairs of opposites in his consciousness while using pure reason. |
| **Knowledge** | We understand knowledge to be information acquired from learning or from one's own experience, e.g. through introspection. For the everyday man, knowledge is information that is registered in the brain through the senses. Knowledge is not just about material phenomena, but can also involve the subjective life and esoteric knowledge, e.g. about energies and forces.<br><br>There are three separate types of knowledge for the spiritual worker to consider:<br><br>• 'Theoretical knowledge' comes from people who are writers and speakers on a certain subject, and represent a type of authoritative source. Since these 'authoritative' sources are experienced in the world of thought, the everyday man trusts and accepts it as factual.<br><br>• 'Discriminative knowledge' – this is knowledge where the person uses his finite ego to rationally consider a set of facts and compare them |

| | |
|---|---|
| | against other information. This type of knowledge is employed typically by the thinker or scientist, and allows him to arrive at an intelligent conclusion. |
| | • 'Intuitive knowledge' is a type of knowledge associated with the Spiritual worker and disciple. The disciple as a soul-integrated personality, is thinking clearly, and has been trained to be receptive or intuitive by making connections with the Buddhic Plane in meditation. |
| **Light** | Light is indicative of how much Soul dominance exists in the personality. In esoteric teachings, there are three main sources of light: |
| | 1. **Light of Knowledge.** This relates to educating the everyday man to allow him to become "consciously human". Knowledge is a product of the finite ego and is an impulse that brings light or understanding to areas of consciousness that are in darkness. In the last 200 years, it has sparked the modern Humanism orientation. |
| | 2. **Light of Wisdom.** This light is the sum of learned experiences combined with knowledge. This light involves illumination of subjective realms of meaning or reality. Its stimulation produces "a recognition of spiritual objectives and with a developed ability to make them the molders of public opinion. They will then be the most important group, expressing the culture of the Aquarian Age. |
| | They will set the standard of values for the masses." Alice A. Bailey "Externalization of the Hierarchy". |
| | 3. **Light of Intuition.** When the Service Worker or disciple begins building the Antakarana using the abstract mind, a pathway to the Buddhic Plane opens up. From it flows the intuition and pure reason. This indicates a blending of the |

| | |
|---|---|
| | Soul light with that of the Monad. This relates to the advanced thinkers and disciples. "3. The education of the advanced thinkers, of the disciples and world disciples in applied knowledge, expressed wisdom and esoteric understanding. This group synthesizes all that is available in the other two groups and thus forms the nucleus of the Kingdom of God, of the fifth kingdom which is so rapidly coming into being." Alice A. Bailey "Externalization of the Hierarchy". |
| **Livingness** | When the spiritual seeker is engaged in a service-related activity, he is expressing the Soul's consciousness. |
| | This connection has a radiant quality or "livingness" to it. Originating from the Soul, "livingness" is composed of light and love moving through an individual's consciousness freely in whatever activity he is involved with. |
| | Its qualities are: |
| | • It is a *prompting* energy to practice harmlessness, integrity and compassion with individuals and groups. |
| | • It is an awareness that is a <u>vitalizing</u> energy and a presence always in the background. |
| | • It is seen and felt as a <u>radiance</u> from the Soul that becomes part of his consciousness to allow that higher nature to flow through him. |
| | • As much as the seeker makes the effort and identify with that Soul energy, then he is guided and can set his intentionality from that place. This energy gives him purpose, intention and direction when it is present. |

| | |
|---|---|
| | As much as the spiritual seeker lives for the purpose of the Soul, then he can become that livingness that the Soul radiates. |
| **Lower 18 Subplanes** | The lower 18 subplanes refer to lowest of the 49 subplanes of the Cosmic Physical Plane. These planes represent the combined energies of: |
| | Etheric-Physical. It is the densest of the planes. It encompasses the four lower kingdoms: the human, animal, plant and mineral realms. |
| | The most dense are the fluids, gases and vapors. Slightly further up, man's 5 senses are registered. |
| | Emotional-Astral. This is the registration of emotions, kama-manas and the desire nature. Here, the majority of humanity exists in a world of emotional living with feelings of fear, anger, hatred, selfishness, love, hope, sentimentality, and separtiveness. From an esoteric viewpoint, this plane is characterized by glamour and illusion. |
| | Lower (Manasic) Mind. Also known as the concrete mind. As man develops his mind and becomes a thinker, he orients himself on this level. The main characteristic of the concrete mind is its capacity for "taking things apart", differentiation, criticism, and using the faculty for selfish, or "separative" purposes. |
| | In today's world, the everyday man exists predominantly on the lower 18 subplanes by creating thoughts usually for his own selfish needs and wants. |
| | His wants and desires drive him in virtually in all of his thoughts, emotions and activities. This line of thinking causes much contentious, opposing, and chaotic energy on the physical and astral planes. It is when man moves to a Soul-oriented awareness and expression, that a new and higher rhythm for |

| | |
|---|---|
| | thinking and feeling will commence.

By transforming the conditions on the physical, astral, and mental planes, he can manifest spiritual living in all aspects of life.

For him to attain this higher objective, he must purify his lower mental matter and kama-manasic substance of the desire mind. This entails purification and a reorientation of his mind towards the Soul.

Doing this will help facilitate the 1st Initiation. Thus, his lower 3-Fold nature will have become stabilized in life expression. |
| **Service Worker** | This is a composite term representing the men and women of goodwill also called the "New Group of World Servers". |
| **Love, Energy of** | In the Ageless Wisdom teachings, the "energy *of love*" is expressed through both individuals and groups. For the individual personality, he expresses love first with self-love in a purely selfish expression of self gratification. Later, he will see beyond his own personal needs, and learn to express love through his own personal family or friends, e.g. love for a mate, a sibling or feeling for a close friend. All of these are examples of love as experienced in the lower three worlds.

From the higher levels, love is that driving force that causes our pure Spirit, the Monad to evolve through light (i.e. the mind), and the will-to-good in the lower three worlds. This force of love propels man on a path of discovery as he seeks to demonstrate the three primary aspects of divinity: light, love, and power. |
| **Love-Wisdom** | When the server is giving both intelligently and loving and caring, he is expressing love and wisdom. To the spiritual worker and disciple, love is |

| | |
|---|---|
| | *felt* in the heart and it is also *known* in the mind. When its blended together, intelligent loving occurs. In the Ageless Wisdom teachings this is known as *love-wisdom*. |
| **Lower Energies** | The so called 'lower energies' exist on the lower 18 subplanes of the Cosmic Physical Plane. Examples of these energies are anger, selfishness, fear, lower desire, separtiveness, thinking in dualistic terms, etc., which keep people separated, and in conflict with each other. |
| | The 'separative' energies are limiting in their scope and disallow the person from making an 'unencumbered' connection with the Soul and the higher planes. For those who consciously express these energies, they are representative of those on the path of involution. |
| | In contrast, the Soul represents love, unity, and group consciousness. To offset and transform these limiting energies, the Spiritual worker expresses love, kindness, cooperation, goodwill, inclusiveness and compassion. For those who consciously express these energies, they are representative of those on the path of evolution. |
| **Maya** | Maya refers to conditions of the physical form nature, e.g. addictions, physical carvings, and gluttony. Maya is identified as one of three main limiters in consciousness, which the Spiritual worker must overcome in order to evolve. The other two are glamour and illusion. |
| | Sanskrit, "Illusion." Of the principle of form or limitation. The result of manifestation. Generally used in a relative sense for phenomena or objective appearances that are created by the mind. |
| **Meditation** | In Sanskrit, the word for meditation is 'Shamatha' or peacefully abiding. "Peaceful Abiding" is a description of how the mind is in its true or natural state. When talking about meditation, we are not trying to create a peaceful state per se, but rather |

have a "direct experience" of who we truly are in our natural state.

The practice of occult / esoteric meditation directly connects the meditator

with the Soul through the abstract mind with the purpose of expanding his consciousness. With the meditator conscious of his own inner realm, he must begin building the Antakarana to connect to the higher and and later to the Spiritual Triad.

The term 'occult' meditation infers that the meditator will be encountering various thoughts, and feelings (i.e. emotional energies) and other forces. It is up to him "how" he will deal with them. The esotericist is 'mindful' and conscious of these energies and forces. He will take a mental approach towards his inner world, while completely subduing his emotional reactivity.

When the meditator goes into meditation, it's important for him to identify realistic goals. Some traditions and teachings about meditation encourage a daily review of the self. From this type of analysis, the meditator can become an observer and a wiser person as he knows who he has been and wants to become. This helps to identify his goals.

Daily practice of meditation is a critical part in integrating the Soul's light, and experience with your personality. This is a practice which will ultimately lead to a connection with the Divine. In your practice, you as the meditator are not trying to create a peaceful state per se, but rather recognize the natural state your mind is already in.

Meditation is based on the premise that our mind's natural state is calm and clear. Meditation provides you with a way to train your mind to settle into this state. Meditation provides you with ways to go deeper within the Self for overcoming obstacles.

| | |
|---|---|
| | For this book, the author is endorsing a "formless" meditation, where the meditator experiences the Soul in its natural state. |
| **Mind** | In the Ageless Wisdom teachings, the mind of man is made up of two basic parts: the lower finite ego and the higher abstract mind.<br><br>**Concrete or Conceptual Mind (or Finite ego)**: This is your main faculty for cognition of your life and environment and it functions as the lowest form of the 'thinking' nature. It has the capacity for logical deduction, rationalization, discrimination, reasoning, and discovery.<br><br>The hallmark of the lower mind is that it knows how to "separate" and identify.<br><br>At some point in your spiritual evolution, you will learn through meditation, to register the Soul's intent or impressions by coordinating the use of your mental, emotional, and physical bodies in service of humanity.<br><br>**Abstract Mind** is a bridge that connects the lower three bodies (i.e. the mental, emotional, and physical), the Soul on the higher mental plane, and the Spiritual Triad.<br><br>The abstract mind, via the Soul conveys illumination, impressions, ideas, intuition, Divine love, and pure reason to the lower mind from the Spiritual Triad. These energies can be converted into service related activities on the physical plane.<br><br>This type of connection becomes possible when the personality is aligned with the Soul through meditation, and begins to construct the Antakarana.<br><br>The abstract mind is the faculty cultivated by the personality that can comprehend physical plane reality. |

| Monad | In the Ageless Wisdom teachings, the Monad is pure 3-Fold spirit on its own plane. The unified triad is composed of Atma-Buddhi-Manas, the immortal part of man that reincarnates in the lower kingdoms. The Monad is a central component in the unfolding of the planetary life, and needs to connect with the lower three worlds via the Soul, as its chief agent for conveying life, will and light to the human personality. |
|---|---|
| **Mystical Path** | The mystical path is characterized by devotion to a person or ideal. The Mystic does not necessarily want to know about the experiences in his mind. This is in contrast to the Probationary Path, where the Service Worker 'wants to know' about what he experiences in consciousness. This path precedes the Probationary, and Discipleship paths. |
| | Nearing the end of the path of the mystic, he will begin to yearn for knowledge about the forces and energies that influence him. He will be drawn onto the Probationary Path and after a measure of purification, he will take the First Initiation. |
| **Observer** | In esoteric terms, the observer is one who notes where his consciousness is at any moment, particularly in the subjective realms. At first, the observer will simply be aware of thoughts and feelings. Later, as he deepens his connection with the Soul, he will perceive impressions, and phenomena in his field of vision, but he remains unattached. The observer while in meditation, will observe any hindrances entering his consciousness. There he will decide how to deal with the energies. Also, while in the outer waking consciousness, he can use the intuition. |
| **Occult – Esoteric path** | A person who is consciously focused in his mind implements the path of the occultist and esotericist by wielding and controlling the energies and forces he encounters. |

|  | The occultist knows how to manipulate and use energy and force, and work with matter. With his knowledge, he has to master and control all lower forms of manifestation, and learn the rules whereby the building devas work. |
|---|---|
| **Pairs of Opposites** | On the path of Discipleship, the Soul comes into conflict with the Personality and battle of the pairs of opposites begins. Over time the Soul energy comes to dominate the energies of the lower three bodies.

The ultimate reconciliation of the pairs of opposites is accelerated by the disciple's contact with the Buddhi energy on the path of Discipleship and Initiation. This energy has no duality or pairs of opposites to engage. The duality, still sensed from the lower planes, causes him to want to be past this and finally let it go, as he is learning to embrace the new energy of 'oneness' from the higher planes.

Working with the pairs of opposites is a process that deals with the pull of Soul and the lure of matter of the lower bodies.

By blending the pairs of opposites, a synthesis is attained, and the middle path, or way is revealed. A "dance in consciousness" with opposing forces and energies ensues.

During this process the disciple learns to create a balance within his own nature and that by bringing in the light or the good, he becomes aware of the dark. Through his attraction to matter and form, he recognizes the pulls of both, and that he stands in consciousness between the two great forces. With the dualities clearly in mind, it dawns on him to realize his struggle is between his own selfish will and that of the higher Divine Will. He chooses to stand in spiritual being.

The Dweller on the Threshold becomes potent after the third initiation in its relationship with the Angel of |

| | |
|---|---|
| | the Presence and the pairs of opposites, through discrimination upon the battleground between the integrated personality and the Angel end duality as the soul becomes in full control and at-one-ment takes place. |
| **Plan, The Divine, or the 'Evolutionary Flow' for Humanity** | The Ageless Wisdom teachings present an understanding that Divine inspiration comes from solar, and cosmic sources. This 'inspiration' is a type of knowledge, and energy that is stepped down into what is called the 'Plan'.<br><br>The Plan, also known as the 'Divine Plan,' or the 'Evolutionary Flow for Humanity' is a blueprint of light, wisdom, and love that guides the Hierarchy of Masters, and all Souls. The Plan is not fixed, it is living. It is imparted to the lower four kingdoms as light and registered in the form of principles, ideas and purpose. This infusion of light penetrates the actual substance of the earth, and all beings living upon it. Its purpose is to raise up all the kingdoms, e.g. the Mineral, Plant and Animal into a more spiritual state of being. As light is absorbed, it reconfigures 'living' energy systems and raises the vibrational frequency of man's atomic substance, particularly in his etheric body. |
| **Polarization** | The word 'polarization' has a different meaning in the esoteric context. It refers to the Soul as being focused 'through' a particular center or vehicle. This vehicle from the Soul's viewpoint is considered to be the clearest channel for communication.<br>Polarity indicates the clarity of the channel. |
| **Pranayama** | Sanskrit: Pranayama is the action of controlling of the vital forces, i.e. prana in the body. Prana or pranic energy is responsible for the life force in the etheric body. The rhythmic inflow of prana through the regulation of the breath will go a long way for achieving a healthy body and mind. |

| | |
|---|---|
| | Regulation of prana, breath control, one of 5 outer limbs of Yoga. |
| **Probationary Path** | The probationary path begins when the person leaves the mystical path. He will begin to study the nature of energy and force, while consciously inquiring about how, and why situations happen in his life. |
| | He begins a purification of his lower bodies by letting go of addictions. |
| | He will begin a preliminary spiritual study of Maya (physical cravings), Glamour (emotional-astral), and illusion (mental) on the Probationary Path. |
| | He practices responsibility, goodwill, and cooperation in his life's encounters. He begins to see and understand the importance of bringing harmlessness and selflessness to service-related activities. Through these efforts he sets himself on the side of the forces of evolution and works at building his character in the image of the Soul, and its higher values. |
| | As a result, the casual body is purified and becoming a receptacle for the Christ-principle. |
| **Purification** | This is an ongoing and necessary process that the student must do to eventually be at-one with the Divine. Purification will entail removing anything from your consciousness that keeps you from realizing God or the Divine. |
| | In the early stages, it will entail you watching your thoughts, practicing harmlessness and leading a virtuous life not just in physical outward practice, but in your consciousness as well. |
| | For the personality, it relates to the physical, emotional, and mental levels of consciousness. |

| Responsibility | A man may be responsible before he embarks on the spiritual path. When the spiritual man begins to expand his consciousness, he will discover there is a direct correlation between how he expresses his personal power, e.g. through his words (as energy) and his actions (his Will as a force).<br><br>Responsibility can be measured by the amount of self-consciousness developed in the man's mind. As one becomes more mindful of the people around him and his surroundings, he must become conscious to have the 'right' attitude to do the 'right' thing and practice harmlessness in all that he does.<br><br>This also infers a selfless 'not thinking of me' approach in serving the higher good. |
|---|---|
| Sacrifice | Sacrifice is about letting go of those aspects of the personality, which are not aligned with the Soul's nature. It is the concept of releasing those impurities, e.g. addictions and lower cravings, that keep us from fully knowing our higher spiritual nature. The everyday man identifies with his material-form nature and wants to hold on to 'things.' This can be anything, e.g. material objects, habits, certain activities, beliefs, and mental / emotional attachments. The personality has both a desire (emotional attachment) and a thought (mental concept of possession) associated with his attachment.<br><br>The lesser man will say: *"this thought or thing is mine"*, and identifies with its possession. From the spiritual point of view, this mindset represents a misidentification of how the mental and emotional energies are held and creates 'separation' in consciousness. Instead, the spiritual man will sacrifice and let go of anything in consciousness that keeps him from fully experiencing his own Soul-nature, and in so doing makes a complete |

| | adherence to the will of God. |
|---|---|
| **Selfishness** | That feeling and personal expression associated with the separated self. It is a state of mind where the 'I' or separate self dominates the consciousness and only considers its own needs. |
| **Selflessness** | Selflessness is related to the spiritual man's ability to serve without any personality concerns or ambitions. To do this he decentralizes his own interests, material, mental, and emotional. |
| **Service** | Service can be briefly defined as the 'spontaneous effect of Soul contact'. This type of contact allows the Soul to pour through man's personality as he is holding a 'spiritual awareness of the Soul' in his heart and mind.<br><br>True service is a life demonstration and based on correct thinking or clear seeing.<br><br>The spiritual man serving humanity and his fellow man is characterized by:<br><br>'Right motive', a pure heart, urge to bring forth the Soul, practiced selflessness, and the forgetting of the personal self. |
| **Service Group** | Members of a *service group* can be part of an outer plane service organization, for example OXFAM, the World Health Organization. Service members are largely made up of the New Group of World Servers who are a group of Spiritual workers, disciples, and initiates of goodwill. They work in all fields of human activity from politics to science, the Arts, education and Healing, and are subjectively linked in helping to manifest the Plan.<br><br>A service group can also be part of an Ashram. With that type of group, they will gather members from the ranks of initiates, disciples and spiritual workers. Each will be accepted into the inner Ashramic group by the Master to fulfill certain requirements of the |

| | |
|---|---|
| | Master's chosen work. The motive to serve must be selfless and harmless. |
| **Soul** | The Soul is the vehicle or 'agent' of the pure Spirit or the Monad. It exists as an intermediary between the Monad and the lower personality. Over lifetimes, the Soul guides man's spiritual development and growth through experiences by expanding his consciousness within the personality. This process is designed to awaken and facilitate spiritual transformation. The Soul is made up of the vital body, the mind stuff and the emotional nature. |
| | The Soul is made up of the vital body, the mind, and the emotional nature. Its known as the Son of Mind, the Ego, the Thinker, or the Christ consciousness. Its purpose is to form a bridge between the personality and the Spiritual Triad, so the Monad can eventually control the life in the lower planes. Expressing the 2nd Aspect Love-Wisdom energy of the Solar Logos, it teaches man how to love like a Soul. |
| | Characteristics of the Soul: |
| | • The Soul being neither spirit not matter but relates the two together. |
| | • The Soul is the source of the quality and characteristics of life. It is responsible for the latent powers of expression in man. |
| | • The Soul contributes self-consciousness and awareness for the form in its environment. Through progressive integrations of the bodies of expression, the consciousness expands. |
| | • The Soul represents the principles of sentiency and intelligence in its lesser reflection of man. This is demonstrated through the mind and mental awareness. This gives man the power to discriminate, analyze, distinguish, and decide. |

| | |
|---|---|
| | The Soul is immortal until the 4<sup>th</sup> Initiation. At that time its causal body is destroyed and it disintegrates. Over the millennia, it incarnates through a personality. When a particular life is completed its purpose, it returns to egoic levels. The immortal Soul provides continuity between successive incarnations by gaining experience and enables the Soul to evolve its consciousness. |
| **Soul-Integrated Personality** | The process of Soul integration occurs by expanding one's consciousness and attaining, stage by stage, ever more inclusive awareness. By connecting with the higher mind of the Soul, and through sustained esoteric meditation, the gap between the lower bodies and the higher mind of the Soul will be bridged. |
| | This brings the disciple's personality into a higher realm of contact and awareness and will result in a soul-integrated personality. |
| | The conscious worker in this context, has a considerable understanding of the nature of energy (focused emotions and thoughts) and force (Will) through the practice of meditation, and spiritual study. His life and consciousness through meditation and applied livingness, demonstrates that he is bringing the Soul's light into his mind with intentionality, while outwardly manifesting this reality as focused service. |
| | By his focus he is in the process of *becoming*. |
| | He has undergone considerable purification, and the Soul has established a considerable influence over his personality tendencies. |
| | At the latter part of this phase, the spiritual seeker will undergo initiations. These are basically expansions of consciousness where the personality is transformed to become soul-integrated. |
| | |

| Soul Urge | The Soul on its own plane will on occasionally make contact with its lower reflection, the personality. This is the development of a 'mental' orientation. Over time, the personality learns to develop a capacity for listening to the Soul's impulses, or urges through impressions, dreams and through stimulation of the etheric centers. |
|---|---|
| Spiritual Triad | The Spiritual Triad is often referred to as the 'Higher Mind' and is a physical expression of the Monad. Technically, the triad composed of the following substance: <br><br> • Atma - The atmic is the plane that is the source of eternal ideas, archetypes, and principles. <br> • Buddhi - Buddhi is the first of the formless worlds, and is the carrier of ideas that are accessed through the intuition. <br><br> • Manas - Manas means 'mind' and refers to the higher part of the mental plane. <br> In contrast, the lower triad or personality is composed of the physical, astral and lower mind. It is the Soul, through the abstract mind that creates a connection between the two triads. Late in the development of the Soul, the personality will create a bridge or Antakarana between the abstract mind and the higher Manas. This will allow the intuition and pure reason to easily flow. <br><br> It is important to note that the mind is that plane which is common to the two triads, and is thus the key to bringing higher knowledge down to earth. <br><br> As these two triads come together, they are understood through the mind. |
| Stages of Evolution | The stages of evolution directly involve man in an 'evolution of consciousness.' |

This evolution is an ongoing process of emotional purification and mental discovery, which can last lifetimes. It involves the spiritual man learning how to control and transform his lower tendencies to a higher and more expansive perspective. The 'lower tendencies,' e.g. selfishness, greed, lower desire, and anger shape our character. They act as hindrances that keep us concentrated in our emotional-astral bodies for a long period of time.

The basic stages of the Spiritual Path, as described by the Tibetan, Djwhal Kuhl are:

- Mystical Path – This is the path of devotion and idealism towards a person, ideal or teaching. This person may be able to reach higher realms of consciousness, but is *not necessarily interested in how to describe it*, or how to return to it.

- Probationary Path - In this stage, the Service Worker takes the first serious steps for treading the spiritual path by beginning to demonstrate control over the basic tendencies of the emotional-astral-emotional body, and physical cravings.

- This is a path of purification and involves the Service Worker demonstrating control over his lower tendencies.

- When he shows a measure of control over his lower self and its tendencies, he will have taken what is called the First Initiation.

- Path of Discipleship (or Esotericism) –This path is characterized by a shift from an emotional focus of the personality, to a mental one. At this stage, most of the astral tendencies are largely under control, and not dominated by the lower consciousness.

| | |
|---|---|
| | Nearing the end of this stage, this personality will have completed the Second Initiation.<br><br>• Path of Initiation - There are five distinct initiations before becoming a 'Master of the Wisdom.' Each initiation is centered around crisis, involving a definite expansion of consciousness. The Path of Initiation involves the expansions of consciousness for the third, fourth and fifth initiations. |
| **Subtle Activism** | Subtle activism is a tool for the spiritual worker to use on the subtle planes. It is a term for spiritually based practices already widely practiced by millions of people, e.g. through meditation, prayer, chanting, sacred dance, ritual, ceremony and any activity designed to bring about change and group transformation. |
| **Tension** | Tension is a type of energy which tells us to *'evolve, move and change.'* The Tibetan D.K. describes tension as the "fixed, immovable Will".<br><br>For the everyday man, it frequently translates into personal change and crisis. While the spiritual man is on the Path and connected to his Soul, he will undergo numerous tests and crises in consciousness. He will discover within himself his own felt point of tension usually from the Soul or other higher guides. He consciously, and through a specific focus of the personality or intentionality, causes himself to move through crisis until the felt tension transforms.<br><br>The discussion about tension is generally in two parts:<br>1. First, there's the tension that does not necessarily have a spiritual component.<br><br>This would simply be the general focus of one's lower consciousness that drives man to perform different activities in his daily life, e.g. the need to earn a living, feed oneself, take care of the |

|  | family, etc. For this, he has a particular tension and focus in his personality 'to do, 'to go,' and 'to make happen.'<br>2. There is 'spiritual tension,' which is the identification of the brain and Soul with the Will aspect to enable a higher purpose. It is the holding and identification of that Will that is the tension. |
|---|---|
| Thought | A single thought is concentrated and materialized thought which is created in mind, and made up of physical substance. Once the thought is constructed, it expresses its will or motivation through physical plane activity under certain rules and laws.<br><br>Combined, it is a unity of thought and force that exists with an expressed purpose. |
| 3-Fold Personality | The human personality evolves through various stages. It is composed of three main parts: mental, emotional, and physical. The everyday person does not necessarily see any relationships or importance of these bodies operating as a 'whole'. The esotericist on the other hand, sees the three bodies functioning as a single integrated unit and, as a useful tool for service.<br><br>Through meditation and cooperation with the Soul, an integration between the Soul and the personality is created known as the 'Soul-integrated-personality.' This allows the integrated personality to become fully 'Soul conscious'.<br>Later, in the advanced initiations, the personality completely disappears and only the pure Spirit, or Monad remains. |
| Transmutation | Transmutation is a process of taking those material energies, either physical or emotional in nature and converting them to into something more spiritual. Since the majority of forces and energies in the material world happen in the astral and dense physical planes, it is the task of the spiritual worker |

| | |
|---|---|
| | to learn to move these up to the level of the mind where he can deal with them dispassionately. At this point, the personality has a relative connection with his Soul as he is still strongly identified with his physical and emotional nature. He is a 'probationer' and developing an obedience to the Soul's impulses.<br><br>When he encounters an emotion or selfish thought, he learns to 'transmute' the energy from selfishness into aspiration, and thus making it a life-giving practice. If the energy is desire, he will transmute the desire energy into love and applied service. |
| **Understanding** | Understanding is the faculty that the thinking man applies to transform knowledge into wisdom. When man is observing and experiencing something of the form nature, he notes that wisdom demonstrates the spiritual effects on the subjective side. Understanding is the link, and relationship between wisdom and knowledge through the insight of the Soul, as the higher thinker. We can also observe that understanding provides a channel for inspiration from the higher levels down to the intellect in the finite ego.<br><br>The energies of understanding, goodwill, love and tolerance allow for disciples to identify on all levels, through synthesis with all forms. |
| **Wisdom** | Wisdom is connected with 'perceiving' or comprehending insights arrived at through interactions and realizations with events, people and situations using the mental, emotional and physical bodies. It deals with the essence or life aspect of things and not with matter by itself.<br><br>As man progresses in his spiritual work, he will see wisdom as a natural outgrowth of the combination of knowledge, interpretation and understanding. Through this perception, the light of the Soul will illuminate his mind. |

# Bibliography

The following books were used as a reference material for the creation of this book:

Alice A. Bailey, *A Treatise on White Magic*, Eleventh Printing, 1977, Lucis Publishing Company New York

Alice A. Bailey, *Discipleship in the New Age, Vol.I*, Tenth Printing 1981 (3rd Paperback Edition, Lucis Publishing Company New York

Alice A. Bailey, *Discipleship in the New Age, Vol.II*, Fourth Printing 1972, Lucis Publishing Company New York

Alice A. Bailey, *Esoteric Healing,* Sixth Printing, 1971, Lucis Publishing Company New York

Alice A. Bailey, *Esoteric Psychology Vol. II*, Sixth Printing, 1971, Lucis Publishing Company New York

Alice A. Bailey, *Externalization of the Hierarchy*, Seventh Printing 1982, Lucis Publishing Company New York

Alice A. Bailey, *Glamour, A World Problem*, Fourth Printing 1971, Lucis Publishing Company New York

Alice A. Bailey, *The Soul, The Quality of Life,* Third Printing 1983, Lucis Publishing Company New York

Aart Jurriaanse, *Bridges – Ancient Wisdom Revealed*, Revised Edition 2001, Bridges Publishing Hans-Juergen Maurer, Freiburg Germany in cooperation with "Sun Centre" School of Esoteric Philosophy, South Africa

Brett Mitchell, *World of the Soul*, First Edition 2002, Esoteric Publishing, Escondido, California

David E. Hopper, *The Soul Source*, Create Space Publishing, Tempe, Arizona 2017.

David E. Hopper, *Glossary of Esoteric Thought*, Create Space Publishing, Tempe, Arizona 2021.

Leoni Hodgson, *Astrology of Spirit, Soul and Body*, 2018

Walter D. Pullen, *Evolution of the Spirit*, 2010 Ozark Mountain Publishing, Huntsville, Arkansas.

William A. Meader, *Shine Forth* – The Soul's Magical Destiny, 2004, Source Publications, Mariposa, California

William A. Meader, *Supernal Light A Compendium of Esoteric Thought*, 2022, Emergent Light, Beaverton, OR

---

References on the Seven Rays:

Alice A. Bailey, *Esoteric Psychology Vol. I + II*, Lucis Publishing Company New York.

Alice A. Bailey, *The Rays and the Initiations*, Fifth Printing 1976, Lucis Publishing Company New York.

Alice A. Bailey, *The Seven Rays of Life, First Printing 1995,* Lucis Publishing Company New York.

Alice A. Bailey, *The Seventh Ray: Revealer of the New Age, First Printing 1995,* Lucis Publishing Company New York.

Helen S.,Burmester, *The Seven Rays Made Visual,* First Edition 1986, DeVoss and Co. Publishers, Marina del Rey, California.

William A. Meader, *Supernal Light*– A Compendium of Esoteric Thought, 2022, Emergent Light, Beaverton, Oregon.

Made in the USA
Las Vegas, NV
27 January 2024

84956609R00138